COMING HOME

COMING HOME

A HANDBOOK FOR EXPLORING THE SANCTUARY WITHIN

BETSY CAPRIO
THOMAS M. HEDBERG

PAULIST PRESS

Acknowledgments
The publisher gratefully acknowledges the use of the following materials:

1800 Woodcuts by Thomas Bewick and His School and *Picture Sourcebook for Collage and Decoupage* edited by Edmund V. Gillon, Jr., both published by Dover Publications Incorporated, 180 Varick Street, New York, New York 10014.

"Cloudy," copyright © 1966 by Paul Simon and "Homeward Bound," copyright © 1966 by Paul Simon. Used by permission.

"Our House" by Graham Nash. © 1970 Broken Bird Music. Used by permission. All rights reserved.

"Hosea" from the album LISTEN © 1973. Composer, Gregory Norbet O.S.B. The Benedictine Foundation of the state of Vermont, Inc., Weston, VT.

"This Alone" by Tim Manion. © 1981 by Timothy Manion and North American Liturgy Resources, 10802 N. 23 Ave., Phoenix, AZ 85029. All rights reserved, used with permission.

Cover art and interior design by Gloria C. Ortíz

Library of Congress
Catalog Card Number: 85-61739

ISBN: 0-8091-2739-3

Published by Paulist Press
997 Macarthur Boulevard
Mahwah, N.J. 07430

Printed and bound in the United States of America

CONTENTS

Introduction   1

Part One: Home . . . Sweet Home
A powerful image

1. *Our Outer Home*   9
   The longing for home • Being without a home •
   Alternative homes • Personal Journal Pages:
   My experience of home

2. *Our Eternal Home*   29
   The great scriptural theme • The primeval
   home • The promised land • The longing for
   Jerusalem and the temple • Jesus and home •
   Paradise regained: The heavenly kingdom •
   Personal Journal Pages: Heaven, for me

3. *Our Inner Home*   45
   The kingdom of heaven is already here • The
   inner home as mandala • Peaceable kingdom,
   garden of love, spring of abundant water •
   Who will dwell in the house of the Lord? •
   Personal Journal Pages: The house in my
   heart

Part Two: Homeward Bound
The most sacred passage of all

4. *The Long and Winding Road*   79
   Two ways to travel • A map for the journey •
   "You will show me the path of life" •
   Personal Journal Pages: Getting ready for
   the trip

5. *How Do We Come Home?*   107
    Searchers for hidden treasure • Tools and
    skills for the journey • Personal Journal
    Pages: Charting the path • Some added
    thoughts

6. *Whom Will We Meet on the Way?*   159
    The inhabitants of the psyche • Room at the
    inn for all • . . . And even the animals •
    Personal Journal Pages: A family portrait

Part Three: Home, at Last
There's no place like home

7. *A Picture of Home*   189
    Land of rest • A map of the soul: our soul-
    scape • Owning our own home • Personal
    Journal Pages: "Go, rebuild my temple"

8. *A Picture of the Homebody*   215
    The shiny person • "You have made us little
    less than the angels" • Wings • Personal
    Journal Pages: Times I've taken wing

9. *Enjoying Our Home*   241
    The house built upon rock • Sharing our
    home • Two great patterns • Personal Journal
    Pages: I will walk in the land of the
    living

In Summary   263

Notes   266

My Favorite Pictures and Quotes about HOME   274

About the Authors   278

Dedicated to
our parents, who first taught us of home:
Robert Bernard and Catherine Nolan Hedberg
and
Arthur Bryan and Jane Blair Whitworth

HOME \hōm\ [OE *hām*] *n* **1**: one's fixed place of abode; the family residence **2**: hence, a place or abode of affection, peace, and rest; a congenial abiding place <He found a *home* in his heart.>

—**at home 1**: in one's own house, place or country **2**: at ease, as if in familiar surroundings

—**coming home 1**: the return to the place of origins, such as a dwelling place or country **2**: the feeling of being in the right place <When he went to see her, it was like *coming home.*>

See also **HOME BASE, HOMEBODY, HOMECOMING, HOME COOKED, HOME GROWN, HOMELESS, HOME LIFE, HOME-LOVING, HOMEMAKER, HOME OWNER, HOMESICK, HOMETOWN, HOMEWARD BOUND**

Introduction

Betsy: Since there are two of us involved in *Coming Home*, we'll each share a little with you of how this book came to be. For myself, it is the most up-to-date statement about my lifelong search for the answer to the question, "What are we doing here?" Since my early teenage years, which would have been in the late 1940's, it has seemed to me that the very worst fate would be to lie on one's death bed and have to say, "Oh no, it's all over—and I never did find out what people are for." I was moved deeply upon first reading Abraham Maslow's description of *meaninglessness* as a "deficiency disease." Later, I felt these words of *The Little Prince*'s author, Saint-Exupéry, to be my words:

> "No one ever helped you to escape (the dismal prison of meaninglessness) . . . Nobody grasped you by the shoulder while there was still time."[1]

The story of my searching would be another book . . . so I won't give you details here. Let it suffice to say that, for many years, the

faith of the Christian church has been my place to find those answers . . . and yet, I have longed for an overlay to that faith that would make it more personal, less collective.

When I read John Sanford's wonderful book *The Kingdom Within* in the mid-1970's, I knew I had that missing link. He, an Episcopal priest, had walked the same path I was on, but several years earlier. Now he shared his understanding of how the very spiritual psychology of C. G. Jung of Zurich had just the sort of individual ingredients for which I was hunting. As I read *The Kingdom Within*, the pictures he described with words kept coming to me visually—in dreams, off the pages of books and television, everywhere I turned. I wanted to get the material he had explored so thoroughly into some sort of visual form. Most especially, I felt the need to share this life-transforming knowledge in a way that the beginner in depth psychology could find usable (a goal which carries with it the problem of *over*simplification).

My first attempt to do so was about 1976, an unpublished book for young people, *Maps of Growth*. The second go at it was an article for *The St. Anthony Messenger* titled "Inner Passages" (February, 1978)—and that seemed a little closer to what I was trying to do, although it had a chart rather than pictures. The third shot at this blending of Christianity and Jungian psychology was a manuscript I played with and shared with anyone who would read it, also titled "Inner Passages." It was half-finished and on a back burner, in need of more maturity on my own part, when my co-author happened along . . . and I will let him take the story from there.

There's just one special thanks that needs to be expressed before I close this more personal part of the book. That is to my mother and father, who—more than any people I've ever known—have had such a wonderful sense of the meaning of *home*. Both were native Virginians. They met in New York City, married and lived there all their lifetime together . . . and yet, home was never far from their thoughts and words; each summer, we would make an annual pilgrimage to the south, to Home (and the capital "H" is appropriate, for there was, to them, no other spot deserving of that name). This was the central event around which their lives circled and which gave their lives meaning. This was the atmosphere in which I grew up and is, I am sure, the reason why—when I went, once more, to write about the subject that had captured my mind

2

and heart for almost forty years— it was the image of *home* that surfaced as most representative of the kingdom within (there are many other metaphorical ways of talking about the kingdom, as you already know and as the following pages witness to).

You, our reader, will appreciate God's goodness when I tell you that, as this book was begun, I became a homeowner (externally, that is) for the first time in my life. The dwelling from which this book has been written, a 1920's Spanish-style house in Los Angeles (complete with white picket fence and trellis and a rose garden), was a completely unexpected blessing I never thought possible. I am supposed to live the image of home on the outside as well as inwardly, it seems. So, the outer mirrors the inner and the inner mirrors the outer—both in the pages that follow and in my own life. And now, my co-author. . . .

Tom: My memories of home go back, especially, to my grandmother's house. This dear woman lived in a small white stucco house in Venice, California (named for the far grander Italian Venice).

The spot everyone was pulled toward was the breakfast nook where there would be fresh flowers from Gram's garden to go with her baked apples. Out back she had canaries, at least two dozen delicate yellow birds singing in the big, old-fashioned wooden aviary attached to the garage. As a child, I never knew anyone else with exotic birds, and it gave going to Gram's something of the feel of going to a fairy-tale cottage for my three brothers and little sister and myself.

However, many of my growing-up years were spent away from this home and my own parents' home—my father's "dream house on a hill." I think it was the away-from-home quality of so much of my early life that has especially made me prize this image. For myself, absence really did make the heart grow fonder; the longing for home began in my boyhood.

In the mid-1970's I came across a book titled *Experiments in Prayer*, then soon found its companion volume, *Experiments in Growth*. As I read the pages about helping religious education come alive for students as bored as my high school charges, I found myself asking "Who is this lady who stole my ideas?" Ten years later, Betsy and I met when her brother-in-law, Fr. Al Caprio, O.P. came from South America to learn about the Y.E.S. programs being pioneered in southern California by several priest-friends and myself. (Y.E.S. stands for Youth Encounter Spirit, and we know from many years of experience that lives are changed when young people of all ages go through the weekend processes we have worked out.)

Betsy and I found we both were working at translating the complex and erudite thinking of C. G. Jung into Christian terms that typical parishioners could grasp; we are both religious educators at heart, as was the founder of my Salesian family, St. John Bosco. Both of us had been moved by the writings of John Sanford, Morton Kelsey and Robert Johnson. We each were looking for ways to experience the Christian message more fully and personally in our own lives, and had turned to analytical psychology for help with the "how" of that: dream-work, active imagination, journal keeping, sandtray images and all the rest of the Jungian methodology. When I saw Betsy's *Inner Passages* work, I said—again—"This is what I've been trying to do too," and knew it should finally be born.

What you hold now is the result of our separate and joint search for our own inner homes. May it be a blessing to its readers as the searching has been a blessing to its authors. Throughout *Coming Home* our readers will find personal stories, contributed by many, many friends and acquaintances. Here is a joint story from us:

"While Coming Home was being born, both of us had occasion to visit old houses in which we once had lived. In fact, we went out of our way to experience these homecomings.

One of the houses, a three-story nineteenth century Victorian building in New England, is falling apart. At this writing it looks as though it might stand no more than half a year or so. No one occupies it; no voices echo through its halls and rooms. It is a ghost house.

The other is a builder's dream house of the 1950's, standing on a hillside in southern California. Once rustic and beige, it has now been made formal by new owners. Elegant landscaping surrounds its imposing dark blue walls; sentry lions guard the front door. It is a foreigner's home.

We experienced nostalgia for the homes that were, the homes in which we once lived—then, slowly, realized that they are still with us. Their rooms and views and furnishings live in our hearts and our memories . . . and, most important of all, because there is within each of us another home we can say our goodbyes to these outer homes without regret. They have taught us about something else."

Together we thank the many who read and advised as this book unfolded. They include our friends Carol Anderson, Neil Bezaire, Cassi Bassolino, Margaret Anne Dickie, Connie Steiner, Sr. Rose Marie Tulacz, S.N.D., and Betsy's daughter Cecelia Kirts, as well as all those who were kind enough to give us feedback on earlier versions. We're especially grateful to the many people whose personal stories appear, anonymously, in these pages. Special thanks to Dr. Meredith Mitchell of Los Angeles, and Salesian fathers Carmine Vairo and Chris Woerz, as well as the staffs of Youth Encounter Spirit and St. Joseph's Youth Renewal Center in Rosemead, California and American Martyrs parish in Manhattan Beach, California. From this parish's fine staff, Emmy Lee and Father Jerry Wilkerson deserve special thanks. Maria Maggi of Paulist Press and freelance artist Gloria Ortíz have worked with us patiently on both this book and its companion manual, and we are grateful to them.

Peace be with you,
Tom Hedberg, S.D.B.
Betsy Caprio

Los Angeles
February 1985

Part One

Home... Sweet Home

CHAPTER ONE

Our Outer Home

The Longing for Home

We all have memories of home. All of us know the longing for home.

The theme is one of the ever-present threads running through our lives.

We meet it in

- our songs

- our stories

- our television shows

- our poetry

9

We open magazines and newspapers and find there the images of people returning home, especially at holiday times.

Two of the most popular movies ever made are saturated with the longing for home:

In *Gone With the Wind*, the recurring theme is Scarlett O'Hara's love for Tara, a love which enables her to take on Yankee armies and greedy carpetbaggers alike.

Over forty years later, the alien *E.T.* longed for his home, not in Georgia but in deep space.

Home is the hunter, home from the hills . . .

No matter what sort of home a person may have had, the condition of nostalgia for home—and even homesickness—is a universal condition, one all peoples of all times and places have

shared. If our childhood home has been a happy one, that may be the home which keeps drawing us back. If not, we may be full of the desire to create a new home of our own, one that will fulfill all our fantasies of "ideal home."

We are the direct descendants of the generations of Americans who came to the New World in search of a home. The history of this nation can, in fact, be told through the stories of those who were looking for a perfect place in which to settle.

People have always dreamed of their own home, even if that place be just a log cabin. "Be it ever so humble, there's no place like home . . ."

10

"The summer of my junior year in high school, I worked for my father's construction firm. That year, he was building 114 houses in Torrance, California— three and four bedroom ranch houses, in about five different models.

I remember very clearly the day I was sorting lumber and the local milk delivery man drove up in his white milk truck. Our construction site was on his regular route, and he had seen the houses going up. He was a big, energetic man with a dark moustache, and he came by every day after that. Soon he started to bring members of his family to see 'the beautiful houses' and then he began to ask questions about costs and loans and payments.

We knew he wanted to own one of the homes, but it looked as though he wouldn't be able to afford such an investment. Now, my father was convinced that it was important for a family to own its own home, if that were at all possible. I can still hear him saying, 'It gives you a sense of dignity and belonging.'

What happened was that my father made some very special concessions for this man so that he and his family could own their own home. They picked out an especially nice one with a brick fireplace I had helped to build, and his happiness and gratitude were something I'll never forget. I remember him saying to me, 'God will bless your father. He is a great man. He made it possible for us to own our own home.'

I've never gotten over the impression this man made on me, and his deep sense of satisfaction at being able to provide a home for his family. I hope they enjoyed it to the fullest and are still there."

Real estate people call this seemingly innate desire "the white picket fence syndrome," and know that much of their time will be spent with lookers-at-houses who really don't intend to buy—but who want to imagine what sort of home they *might* fancy.

Many of us are those weekend house-hunters who comb the newspaper ads for the house of our dreams, and visit each and every open house. It's another way to satisfy the longing we seem to have for a home. This hunger starts young: dollhouses and sets of blocks are the pre-schooler's ways of creating a home, as is laying out sticks or rocks on the ground in a miniature floor plan.

It's a hunger our animals know about too. What cat-owner has not found Kitty curled up in some special spot to which she has declared eminent domain? And we build dog houses for our dogs, bird houses for our birds, even homey underwater environments for our fish that are often tiny replicas of human dwellings.

Our favorite characters from fiction almost always have a home base which seems an essential part of their personalities:

- Sherlock Holmes has his "digs" at 221-B Baker Street in London.

- Dorothy could never have stayed in Oz. She needed her Kansas farm home far more than the Emerald City.

- even the adventurers of *Star Trek* have a home base to which they regularly return: the *U.S.S. Enterprise*.

This longing for home is a universal need, part of everyone's life. It seems to be built into us at some deep and hidden level.

HOME ▷

"I'm a little embarrassed to tell you this story—it's so silly, but it's true. When I was fifteen, I had a boyfriend named Marty, and I just thought he was wonderful. He was the end on the high school football team and was real cute, except that he was missing a front tooth which he had lost at the line of scrimmage.

Anyway, we were pretty serious, and we spent hours dreaming about the house we'd build together one day. It even had a name, which I really shouldn't tell you, but I will—we called it 'Housie for Mousie.' (Well, we were fifteen!) He was good at drawing, and we sketched pictures of how it would look, and all sorts of floor plans. We had copies of Better Homes and Gardens and American Home all over the place. My mother was beginning to get antsy! I think she was wondering why we weren't doing 'normal' things, like jitter-bugging on her living room rug.

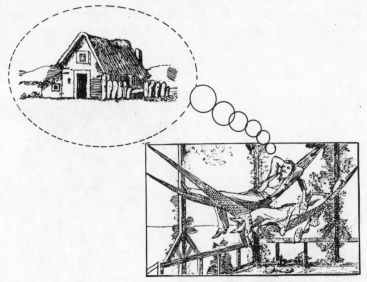

Well, one day Marty and I came to the point of no return. We were designing our future dining room, and had this huge fight about what color the walls would be. I was absolutely set on wallpaper with pink roses, and grey paint for the trim, and he said he would never eat a bite in a room that looked like that. It had to be green grass-texture wallpaper or nothing. . . .and if I didn't like it then we probably didn't have a future together.

Can you believe that we broke up over that? We did. Both of us cared that deeply about what our future home would be like. It just amazes me today that at fifteen I was ready to battle to the death over the idea of home. It must have been a very strong hunger in me, even then . . . and it still is today, thirty-five years later."

Being Without a Home

Not all have a home, though. They may be away from that place
temporarily—
while in the service,
or working on the road,
or permanently—
because they have been forced
to flee their homeland,
or have, perhaps, chosen such a life,
or have seen their home dissolved through
the tragedy of divorce.

And there are many among us who have *never* known a real
home: orphans, perhaps, or those whose habitations were so filled
with strife and loneliness that they didn't come near the meaning of
the word "home."

Whether or not we have actually been without a home, there is
within each of us something of the homeless one, the exile—for we
know that the experience of being a refugee could befall anyone.
We can scarcely bear to look at the pictures of the people uprooted
in Viet Nam or El Salvador. The man or woman without a country
could be ourselves.

15

"There was only one time in my life when I hired a cleaning woman, mostly because I felt uncomfortable having someone else take care of my menial tasks. (Also, I didn't want anyone to see what slobs we were, so I'd rush around cleaning up before she got there—which was sort of stupid!) But the one time was during the 1960's, at the height of the civil rights activity in the south, and it was then that a quiet, tall black woman came to work for me for a few months.

Her name was Jane, and she was from Alabama. I fixed lunch for us the first day she came, and as we ate I said to her, 'Oh, you must be glad to be living in the north now.' (She and her husband had left Alabama not only because of the violence there, but also because they couldn't make a living on their old farm.)

'No,' she replied, very slowly, 'I would give anything to be back in Alabama. That's my home.' It didn't matter to her how it had been for them; she wanted to be home. And at that moment, I felt a wave of nostalgia in my own heart, even though I was at home."

One of the most memorable experiences of homesickness was that shared by millions during the first moon landing, in July of 1969. The American astronauts had achieved their daring vault into space. They had landed their Apollo 11 craft on the moon's surface and planted the flag, then leapt like gazelles in the low-gravity environment. They had collected rock samples and dust samples. They had radioed back their first excited impressions of this distant satellite.

Then, turning back to look in the direction from which they had come, they saw Earth, their home, two hundred and forty thousand miles away. Like a beautiful disc it rose, mist-wrapped, over the moon's horizon. And with the Earth-rise, reported the astronauts, they were swept with a tremendous longing for this home so far away. As they spoke, proud Americans watching the space travelers shared in their emotion, as did Russian citizens and those viewing in South Africa. And had they had television screens before them or radios on which to listen, the most primitive peoples on our globe would have understood this longing for home; the nostalgia of which the space voyagers spoke would have touched hearts in mud huts on the Amazon delta as equally as those in igloos north of the Arctic circle. And all who did follow the journey rejoiced later at the homecoming of the astronauts, as they splashed down safely many hours after their report of yearning for home.

Just as we intuitively know about exile and homelessness—whether or not we have actually lived it out—we also know about the joy of coming home. The word

is used in different ways:

- there are homecoming dances, and football games and queens.

- there are homecoming outreach efforts made by churches and temples and synagogues, urging those who have been "on sabbatical" from the faith of their ancestors to return to their spiritual homes (often called—not by accident—"Mother Church").

- there are the long pilgrimages made by those who seek out the seat of their religious faith, or who go back to visit the old family homestead in the place of their birth. Sometimes these homecomings are disappointing, terribly disappointing, when the pilgrim realizes that "you can't go home again."

In some way, each of us knows what it is to be away from home and to long for it. Just as appreciation of the idea of

is common to all the people who have ever been and who ever will be, so too is the capacity for missing home. It is not just the homeless who are homeless. . . . .

   not just those whose jobs transfer them every two years who
      know rootlessness. . . . .

      not just the many who are crowded into slum apartments
        who have no fit dwelling. . . . .

         not just those in distant lands who are foreigners. . . . .

At a deeper level, being without a home is common to everyone. It is the other side of our appreciation of home.

Alternative Homes

Because being without a home is so much part of the human condition, we seem to have a built-in knack for creating alternative or substitute homes for ourselves. Or, maybe we should say that because the instinct for homemaking is so much part of the human condition, it gets exercised in the creation of micro-homes and mini-homes, as well as dwelling-place homes. It is a talent we have, and one that finds all sorts of ways to express itself.

This alternative home urge is most often expressed by setting apart some small space for ourselves:

- a room of our own, or just a corner or spot in a room

- our car

- a garden patch or a special park

- even a woman's pocketbook or a briefcase ("I live out of my purse")

- a favorite pew in a church or a regular seat in a classroom

People of other cultures have set aside this sort of protected space or sanctuary in the form of

- the cave of the hermit

- the sacred grove of the god or goddess

- the prayer rug which can be spread out on the desert sand to create a miniature garden

Jesus went up on a mountaintop to pray, or pushed out to sea in a boat in order to claim this kind of personal space; these were the alternative homes in his itinerant life.

Another way we re-create the idea of home for ourselves is by carrying with us the things that stand for home:

- a favorite picture

- letters from loved ones

- tapes of favorite songs

- even dirt from the homeland

- the holy book of our tradition

- a childhood toy or treasure

We keep in touch with the people who have been our home base:

- our family

- dear friends, the neighbor who always welcomed us

- the spiritual guide or mentor who made such a difference

- the beloved pet

- the author who speaks just our language, whose books we would not be without because they have become our touchstone

"One of the best compliments I ever received was from the woman I love. One day, when we had been seeing each other for about six months, she said to me, 'Being with you is like coming home.'

I remember thinking, 'What an honor to have someone say I'm able to do that for her.' And, as I thought about it, I knew she did the same thing for me. So I married her!—and now we have a home of our own."

All these alternative homes or things that stand for home help fill the hunger in the human heart for a home of one's own. We set apart special space, we take with us the reminders of home, we stay connected to the homefolk even if we *do* have a house-type home— and if we do not have an outer home, for any of many possible reasons, these substitutes for home become all the more precious to us.

"In 1968, my family and I knew we had to leave Havana. We made all the arrangements, and waited a long time until we could get passage for the six of us on a fishing boat: there was mi esposa *Gloria*, our three little boys, and mi abuelito—you would say 'the grandfather.'

We had planned carefully what to bring with us, and left behind most of our personal belongings so we could carry the Bible with all the names of the family in it and all the dates of weddings and baptisms and funerals. And we brought the big old photograph album, and the large crucifix that my grandfather's grandfather had carved back in the 1800's when Cuba was under Spanish rule.

The night came for our trip to Miami. We had said goodbye to our home. I was trying to be brave so my sons and wife could tear themselves away. We started off down the street to meet the man who had arranged our passage, when suddenly Gloria turned and ran back into our garden. She came back in a minute or two, carrying a wide leaf from the palm tree in front of our house, a tree she had loved and sat under to rock the boys when they were little. It's all brown now, but we have it behind the crucifix right here on our living room wall today."

Log cabin,
   castle in Spain,
      dome in the ice country,
         tent in the desert,
            ranch house in suburbia,
               home on the range. . . . .

Motherland,
   fatherland,
      adopted land,
         land that I love. . . . .

Tiny space that I call my own,
   reminder of a home long gone,
      memories that are all that's left of an outer home. . . . .

Whichever of these is ours,
   Home is, surely, where the heart is.

    The section that follows each chapter has personal journal pages for the reader's own reflections. (If you are sharing this book with a group or class, you may want to copy the blank pages before writing on them.)
    Making the ideas in each chapter our own is the best way to let them become rooted in our lives. Journal recording helps with this sort of grounding.

Personal Journal Pages
My Experience of Home

What associations come to mind when I hear the word "HOME"?

WORDS

SCENES FROM MY LIFE

STORIES/MOVIES/T.V. SHOWS/SONGS

Here are some words people use to describe their feelings about home.

cozy	secluded	warm
happy	open	depressing
crazy	lonely	nourishing
friendly	safe	fun
dark	criticizing	angry
love	friendship	punishing
emptiness	colorful	exciting
chaotic	sheltering	touching
acceptance	rejecting	life-giving
humorous	smothering	laughing
dominating	peaceful	prayerful
confused	violent	cradling
spontaneity	learning	abuse
judging	celebrating	repairing
teasing	clowning	serenity
sacredness	molesting	scolding
stressful	sanctuary	relaxation

Check the five that are closest to my feelings about HOME.

Put an "x" next to those five that are least like my feelings about HOME.

Are there memories of home for me that are not happy—and that still need healing?

Over a period of time, I could relive these memories and bring the Lord into each of them, letting God's healing power put to rest the pain I still feel. This may take some time, as each painful memory may have to be re-experienced slowly, piece by piece. We know we have been healed of past hurt when we can relive a time from our past and be at peace about how it was, even at its worst, believing that God produces good out of all things.

What "alternative homes" or set-apart space have I created for myself during my life?

As a child (hideaways under tables, in trees, etc.)

As an adult (a special corner, my car, etc.)

Do I have a set-apart space in my life now? If not, how could I create one? (a place in my home? being with one other person or a group of special people? a journal that is my own "protected space"? a special church—perhaps even my special spot in that church?)

Have I ever had the experience of feeling HOMELESS?

When?

What was it like?

Thinking back over dreams I have had when sleeping, are any of them about a HOUSE or a HOME? If there are more than one of these dreams, or a series of them, in what way has the image of the house changed and developed as I have grown?

CHAPTER TWO

Our Eternal Home

The Great Scriptural Theme

The bibles and holy books of all the world's religions have the image of

woven through them. It seems that this idea of home is not only powerful for each of us on a personal level, and on a patriotic level, and on a global level (planet Earth as our home), but also at a spiritual level. This is especially true of both Judaism and Christianity, faiths whose holy scriptures are filled with a variety of homes.

The interesting thing we discover is that the scriptural homes all point to something beyond them. They are about a resting place that is

everlasting. . . . .
   unchanging. . . . .
      infinite. . . . .
         timeless. . . . .
            permanent. . . . .

They tell us there is more than the homes—and alternative homes—of this earth. There is an eternal home.

The Primeval Home

Our scriptures open with the creator God fashioning an earthly dwelling place for us. Each step of the process is observed by the creator, and judged to be good. Not content with just one version of creation, the book of Genesis gives us two—and the second story has, in wonderful detail, a word-picture of a garden home, to the east.[1] Artists have brought to life for us its marvelous ingredients:

- "all kinds of pleasant trees," with two special trees in the midst of the garden

- "a river flowing in Eden that watered the garden, separating into four branches"

- "all the beasts of the field, and the birds of the air"

- "God walking in the garden"

This first home of scripture is a place where man and woman can come together and be completely themselves; their humanness is entirely natural to them.

And we, pondering Eden, are left with the same sense of completeness and harmony. . . . the garden of Paradise is a centered place, almost always depicted through the centuries with one or both of its trees in the middle (or sometimes with a shrine to mark the center).

. . . . it is a sanctuary filled with God's presence, around which a
    most peaceful life revolves,
       . . . . it is bounded by the four tributaries of its river, and
        these are invariably drawn flowing to the four directions
          of the compass,
             . . . . and, apparently, the garden has some sort of
               enclosure that sets it apart. Again, the artists and
                 our imagination have supplied a wall and a gate
                   to protect this sacred space, even though these
                   are not mentioned in Genesis.

The bible begins with a perfect home.

"Do you remember that awful joke about Adam and Eve? It's been around forever, and goes like this:

Adam and Eve were trudging down the road from Eden, wearing their fig leaves and pushing a wheelbarrow filled with their dishes and books. Eve was complaining bitterly, 'Adam, we were so happy. You promised me we'd never have to move.'

Adam turned to the flesh of his flesh and said, 'Well, dear, I did, that's true. But you let in one snake and there goes the whole neighborhood!'

Of course, my congregation always greets this one with appropriate groans, but it says something about projection, doesn't it? And it says something about what it's like to have to leave home—my people know about that."

The Promised Land

The garden experience, alas, does not last. No sooner are we caught up and delighted with the totality of Eden than the story goes on to speak of homelessness.

Its inhabitants are cast out. An angel with flaming sword guards the eastern entrance to the garden, the side on which the sun—symbol of rebirth—rises. The tree of life can no longer be reached. Paradise is lost.

Other homes, far less satisfying than the primeval home, are described in the first books of the bible. We hear of temporary homes like Noah's ark, for instance, and are struck by their contrast to the perfect place which preceded it.

And yet, early on, a second home of great joy is beginning to take shape in our minds and in the hearts of the people of these pages:

" . . . a land I will show you . . . a great nation . . . all the land which Abram can see to the north and the south and the east and the west . . ."[2] It is the promised land, which would be given by God to the people of Israel, lost to them, regained by them—over and over throughout the pages which follow.

It is called Canaan and, later, Israel (which may be translated as "let God shine"),[3] and we are told that it is

- a land flowing with milk and honey,

- a land across the Jordan River,

- a fertile and prosperous land, where the palm trees wave.

It is not the garden of Eden regained, but it is home for the people of Israel, the chosen ones with whom God has bonded in a covenant of love. And these people
    fight for their home,
        are fiercely proud of their home,
            and—when in exile from it—mourn
                grievously for their home.

How can we sing the songs of our God when we are far from home?

The Israelites are not the only ones who have sought their promised land. The story has been repeated throughout history, and the sad reverse side of it is that one people's longing for a home often means homelessness for another people; the American Indians know a great deal about this. To value home, we learn in scripture, is to make oneself vulnerable to the pain of *not* having a home. The two go together.

The Longing for Jerusalem and the Temple

From its beginnings, the people of Israel had known their homeland needed a physical center. We read of their determination to create one. The *spiritual* center of these biblical people was the Law which God had given to Moses on Sinai. In their wandering, desert days, the Israelites had encased the tablets of the commandments in the wondrously carved and decorated ark of the covenant, built with great care and carried before them. Even as a homeless people, they had made a tent-dwelling for the ark, a fitting place for God's presence among them.

And, as they became a settled people with their own land and their own kings and queens, it became vital that this sign of God with them have a permanent residence, a home of its own,

> *Build a sanctuary*
> *to the Lord God . . .*
> *a house which is built*
> *in the name of the Lord,*

34

"I remember a time when I was about five, walking in the front door of our Cheviot Hills home in Los Angeles. I was in tears, crying and feeling sorry for myself because I had fallen in a puddle of mud. My mother was always sympathetic to me, but this day she just looked at the mess I had trailed in and said, in her dear Irish way, 'Oh, my God . . . what will your father say when he sees what you've done to the carpet? . . .'

I hadn't thought about that incident for years, until I went to Maui with the Youth Encounter Spirit program. 'Maui no ka oi!', they say, which means 'Maui is the best'—it was the first time I had lived where people took off their shoes before entering their homes, and I was deeply touched by the reverence these beautiful islanders showed for their homes and families. That reverence carried over to their reception of our youth and family programs.

I know that taking off one's shoes before entering a holy place is practiced in many parts of the world by people coming home and going into their temples and shrines, just as Moses took off his shoes before approaching the burning bush. Now, I do the same when I enter my room in our community home, which is a sort of sanctuary for me. It slows me down, and puts me back in touch with what is most important—the sacred.

A fringe benefit of this practice has been that when I go to visit my parents I'm very, very careful about wiping my feet before I walk in the door—their house is holy ground, in more ways than one!"

said King David to his son, Solomon.[4] And Solomon went on to build a temple like none ever built before, a temple of finest gold and precious marble and cedar trees without number. And in the center of the temple was the Holy of Holies, and in the center of this sanctuary was the ark.

"The temple was filled with the glory of God," we read, and once again, hearing these words, we experience the peace that comes to a people who have their house in order, with God at its core. This is a peace that has been missing from the pages of scripture since the garden times.

Now the temple was the heart of the home city of the promised land,

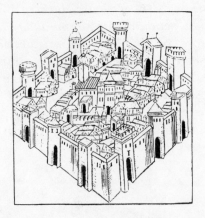

"Jerusalem, O Jerusalem. . . . if I forget you, O Jerusalem. . . ."
City of Dreams, built on Zion,
City of Truth,
City of Joy,
City of God.

The beloved city of the people of Israel is God's delight, we are told.

"Can a mother forget her baby?. . . . Jerusalem—I will never forget you! I have carved you in the palm of my hand!"[5]

Once more, we are drawn into sacred space, set-apart space which is consecrated to God—this time, a walled city. For the Jewish people, the city of Jerusalem stands for home, and they leave each other to this day with the hope of meeting "Next year in Jerusalem!"

Jerusalem is the geographical focal point of scripture. It is at the center of the story; it is also at the heart of several peoples and their longings . . . and these peoples are our ancestors.

Jerusalem, too, is home.

Jesus and Home

Our path through the Bible winds on, pausing briefly at Bethlehem. And, how interesting, artists have elaborated on the very casual mention in the earliest infancy narrative of a house in which Jesus was born, as though they wanted to provide the Son of Man with a place to lay his head . . . a place superior to a manger.

Later we picture Jesus at home in a little house in Nazareth, with Mary and Joseph. Two thousand years of pious tradition have filled in the details of that life for us, details not found in the written word. It is as though we have needed to know about Jesus' home life, knowing that a holy family deserved a holy place, and so we visualize the carpenter's shop and the simple hearth, a flat roof reached by ladder. It too is a sanctuary, made holy by God's presence there.

Then Jesus has left his childhood home, although he is to be called "the Nazarean"—he is named for his home town. He moves quickly through his three years of wandering, giving up a place of his own. "Even the foxes have a den and the birds of the air a nest . . .", but not the Lord. His followers are also homeless, giving up all to follow Jesus.

Yet, he shows us how important home is to him:

- in the famous homecoming parable of the Prodigal Son,

- in his visits to the home in Bethany, where Lazarus and his sisters await him,

- in the home-folks who travel with him and support him, creating a home away from home,

- in his love for Jerusalem and the temple, the home base of his people.

And Jesus reaches back, at his death, to the earliest biblical language, saying that "this day" he will be in Paradise.

Even from the cross, he speaks of home.

His earthly story ends with the transition from one home to another: the Lord of the world leaves this temporal home to go home to God the Creator, who is beyond time and place. He prepares us for our own transition to eternal home. And then, the last pages of scripture are upon us, bringing us a picture of a home that surpasses any we have met so far. . . . .

Paradise Regained: The Heavenly Kingdom

The biblical people, whose homeland was enslaved over and over, whose temple and holy city were destroyed, rebuilt, and destroyed again, at last are given the ultimate, permanent vision of home.

They are shown an eternal home . . . and, looking back, they can see that the earlier scriptural homes have pointed to this one, the best and most beautiful of all!

It is a perfectly symmetrical walled city,
with three gates to the east,
and three gates to the north,
and three gates to the south,
and three gates to the west . . . each made from a single pearl,
    and watched over by an angel.

Precious jewels form the foundation of this heavenly kingdom. Its streets are of gold, and an emerald rainbow surrounds the crystal sea which encloses its centermost treasures:

The Tree of Life

The Lamb of God
on the Throne

The River of the Water of Life

"When I was growing up in Virginia in the 1940's, my parents used to take me to Homecoming Sundays at the Baptist church. They had these every summer, and all the people who had not been churchgoers for a while would make a real effort to return on that day. A special drawing-card was all the good home-cooked foods prepared by the church ladies—fried chicken, biscuits, strawberry preserves, pecan pies.

I remember these well!

And I remember the hymns the people would sing about homecoming too:

"I'm only goin' over Jordan,
I'm only goin' over home."

They were about dying and going to heaven:

"I'm goin' there to see my mother,
I'm goin' there, no more to roam . . ."

Then there were the happier songs. I can still hear lines like "Jerusalem the golden, with milk and honey blessed. . . ." and "Oh happy home, forever blessed, in that dear place how sweet our rest."

All my life I've had such beautiful ideas about heaven. I believe it will be, for me, like coming home."

This celestial city is, truly, the home of God. A perfectly designed sanctuary, it draws us to it with its symmetry and tranquillity. It is the home called "heaven," resplendent with the blessed and the angels—and, most of all, with release from the cares of earthly life.[6]

The way it is described, the heavenly home is like a city from a dream world. It sounds like the storied kingdoms of the fairy tales, where all "live happily ever after"—and, indeed, many of these tales are secularized versions of lives of the saints, whose stories ended when they went home to the heavenly kingdom.

Is this where we too are headed?[7]

Enclosed garden,
    promised land,
        shining temple,
            holy city,
                humble dwelling,
                    celestial kingdom . . .
all, God-filled sanctuaries of peace and symmetry.

The Jewish and Christian and other scriptures, the holy books on which we are raised and nurtured, are saturated with rich images of set-apart sacred space, soul-satisfying pictures of HOME.

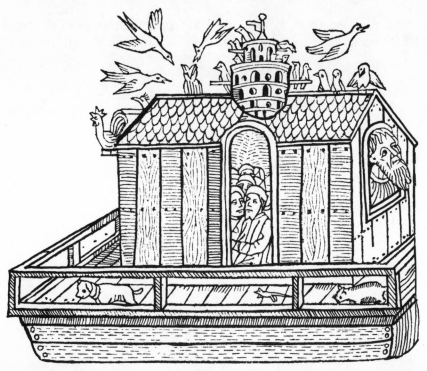

Personal Journal Pages
Heaven, for Me

Which of the scriptural images of home speaks to me most deeply?

What do I most like about this biblical home?

If I were John the Evangelist, setting down in words the picture of the New Jerusalem which we find in *Revelation 21*, what would I include in *my* heavenly city?[8]

What are my earliest memories of how heaven was presented to me (if it was)? What are the sources of these memories?

In my celestial geography, where does heaven seem to be?

Is it "up" or "above," as so often pictured? Have I ever seen pictures of people climbing ladders or staircases to heaven, or holy mountains? Why does the idea of going up or transcending seem to be so widely used to speak of heaven?

Is heaven a "home in the sky" (as the Cat Stevens song has it)? If not, then where is this place—or, is it a place at all? How does it seem to me?

There is a long tradition of seeing heaven as a release from earth—the "vale of tears," in which we are "poor banished children of Eve," or "poor, wayfarin' strangers." Is this how I feel about this life and the afterlife?

CHAPTER THREE

Our Inner Home

The Kingdom* of Heaven Is Already Here

We've seen how, in our lives and the lives of our biblical ancestors, the ideas of

are ever-present and power-filled. For an image to be so potent, it must correspond to something inside us. The idea and images of outer home and of eternal home pluck some chord which is rooted in our deepest soul-level. . . . . an inner idea and image of HOME. Were this not so, we could not respond to external home and scriptural home so strongly. We could not be gripped by them, feel them resonate within us, care about them so dearly.

---

*The word *kingdom* is considered by some to be exclusive of women, a sexist word. While there are many such words that we can well dispose of, your authors do not feel *kingdom* is one of them. We agree with those (like Rosemary Reuther) who remind us that the idea of kingdom has rich levels of meaning and power for all Christians and Jews (and certainly for the Jewish Jesus), levels that the words *realm* or *reign* or *sovereignty* just don't capture. In addition, kingdoms have often been ruled by queens; the word is broader than gender.

All our longing for home and for coming to that home,
   all the pain that goes with being away from home,
      all the creativity we put into establishing alternative homes,
         all the journeying of the biblical people to their assorted
            homes,
is also about our hunger to be in an inner home:

- a garden oasis within us

- a promised land of freedom and peace, close at hand

- a temple of God deep inside our being

- an enclosed city, safe and contained

- a house with many rooms, the recesses of our souls

- a golden city, with many mansions.

This inner home is the kingdom of heaven within us. It is already here, Jesus told us. It is that part of us we cannot see, called *soul* or *psyche* (some use these words interchangeably, others make fine distinctions between them).[1] It is a parallel universe as real and knowable as the everyday world which surrounds us.

Many people seem born to be in touch with this inner world all their lives—in fact, this *is* their real world, informing and giving meaning to the external events they experience. (William James' name for them was "the once-born." Gerald O'Collins calls them "the smooth evolvers";[2] they don't have to be converted to the interior life.)

Others among us are barely aware of this part of themselves; their reality must be touchable or seeable or tastable in order to be believed. Their focus is "out there." And yet, even these people will speak of inner glimpses from time to time: a dream remembered, a childhood time of daydreaming, a peak experience which took them out of themselves—or an abyss experience which did the same. Surely, there must be very few among us who have not at some time experienced this inner terrain.

This kingdom of which Jesus spoke "is not of this world." We carry it within us, a home so often forgotten and neglected that it has become covered over. Many of us are cut off from it, in exile—just like the people of Israel in Babylon. And our hearts are as heavy as theirs, even if we do not know the cause of our dis-ease.

We may busy ourselves with a million external tasks, become very important to countless other people, do all sorts of marvelous things in the outer world. . . . but all the time, the hidden home within is waiting to be uncovered and revealed to us. And the knowing of this inner abode fills the longing for home we have experienced in so many outer ways, fills it in a way that even a mansion in Beverly Hills or a king's palace could not. (How precious the experience of inner home must be *especially* to those of us who are without an outer home.)

"This is a story I still can't quite believe, but it really happened and I want to share it with you. I'm 35 years old, and I have had what's called 'the good life.' It's been great—my family had all kinds of money and I did the 'right things' growing up, went to good schools, married Mr. Right, had two beautiful children—a boy and a girl. We live in this absolutely magnificent house in a suburb of Paris, go to the opera and the Riviera at the best seasons and so on—you get the picture, don't you? (Oh yes, best of all is that I can still wear a bikini and look good!)

Here I was, until two years ago, and in spite of this terrific life something was wrong. I felt so empty, so cut off from myself—and all my friends were the same way, just rushing around doing things, but not knowing why. I kept feeling 'there's got to be more than this.'

I've never paid attention to my dreams, although I know I've always been a dreamer . . . . and then, one morning I woke up very early, before daybreak, with this vivid dream in my mind. It was so real that it made me shake all over. I'll never forget it. This was the dream:

'I'm in my house (I think it was our home) and I see that where the living room wall was there is now an open wall with two archways. On the other side is a room so beautiful—it has white walls, and polished oak floors, and sunlight streaming in through the clean, clean windows (I think they are leaded and with beveled glass, like in the old Victorian houses). There was no furniture, but many green plants all over, all very alive and growing.

'I stand and just look at the room, and know that it is waiting for me to come in and explore it. It's like some holy place; I just don't dare cross over into it. It is very new—but at the same time very, very old.

'Then I notice a door I haven't seen before. It's on the far side of the new room, and begins to swing open slowly. When it's open all the way I can see that beyond this first room are many, many others—all visible somehow through this one door. And they are each a different color—soft colors, like in a rainbow. And some of the rooms have trees growing in them, and others have beautiful art work, and chandeliers made out of crystal and diamonds, and some are very dark so that I have no idea what's in them.

'All the time I'm standing there, it's very clear that the first room and all the rest are my house, and that I'm supposed to go in and live in this house.'

That was the dream. I just can't tell you how even telling it again touches something I've never felt before. Now, I don't know about dreams and all that stuff, but I do know that this dream is about something important to me, something that will fill up the emptiness of my life. Somehow, I have to get to know that house I dreamt about. Oh yes, here's a little picture I drew of the dream. . . . . ''

The kingdom of heaven, said Jesus, lies hidden,
   like a treasure buried in a field. . . . .
      It is, also, like a storage room, filled with
         old things and new things
            waiting to be discovered. . . . .
               Then again, it is like a merchant in search of a fine
                  pearl;
                    it seeks us out and calls us to it. . . . .

         And it is like a mustard seed, good seed that
            spurts up and grows into astonishing
               wholeness. . . . .
The home within us is even like a wedding feast, he told us, the
great celebration of human love. . . . .

And some four centuries before the Parisian dreamer who has
shared her house dream with us, Jesus' friend Teresa said,

*The kingdom
of heaven
is like an
interior castle.*

50

This is the home within us. And because it is real and alive and calling out to us, the idea and images of our outer homes and of the scriptural homes stir us so deeply. We see in them the reflection of the invisible home within.

The Inner Home as Mandala

God the creator has fashioned billions of individuals since time began, each unique—yet each very alike. We have the ancient picture of God as potter, molding each of us. Always, unless something goes wrong with the process, the person emerges with the archetypical human form: a trunk with head and four appendages. Faces may vary enormously. . . . yet still they contain two eyes, a nose and a mouth, two ears, some hair. Each hand, each foot is special—yet, they too conform to the human pattern of five fingers or toes apiece.

And it is this way with the pattern of the soul, too—this inner home that is like buried treasure and a storeroom and a merchant and a seed and a wedding feast. There is a universal form that is imprinted on the soul by the potter-God. It is as universal as the

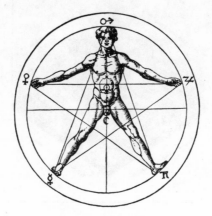

form of the human body, while at the same time allowing for the differences that make no two souls the same.

Our biblical pictures of home tell us about the soul's universal form or blueprint; each is a description of sacred space in a geometrical shape, with a boundary equidistant from a holy center spot:

- in Paradise, the tree of life grows in the center (of most representations), and the four rivers are assumed to head off in four ninety-degree turns of the compass.

- the promised land is shown to Abram as land to the four directions. There is a center here too, the patriarch himself, God-filled. Abram also set up an altar here, as was the custom of his people.

- the temple of Solomon was a rectangle, but careful reading of its description shows it may have appeared square, for its porch (the part which would have been seen first) was as wide as the temple was deep. And even those who never entered the temple knew there was a heart-center to it: the ark of the covenant.

- Jerusalem, built on Zion, had very irregular walls. Yet, by the time Jerusalem shows up in drawings of the early Church, those rendering the holy city have squared her off. The city is wrapped around the temple, which encloses the Holy of Holies, which contains the ark. The Jerusalem in people's hearts *is* symmetrical, because it stands for a place where God lives and peace reigns.

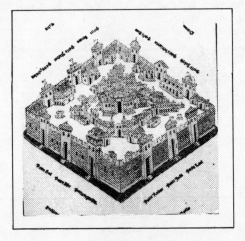

- and, finally, the heavenly Jerusalem of *Revelation*, laid out in perfect symmetry: it is a square with the *living* God at its very center.

Each of these biblical homes takes the shape of a mandala: a holy circle (which may be squared off to indicate that it is being realized)

*—Theophan
the Recluse*

with a centerpoint. The mandala is the universal image of totality and perfection; the word is Sanskrit, meaning "to be in possession of one's essence."

The scriptural homes stand for the home within each of us—and their pattern shows us the pattern of that inner home. The kingdom we contain can, also, be described as "mandalic": symmetrical bounded sacred space with God dwelling at the center, the God who says, "I will come and make my home within you, if you love me and obey my teachings." We carry within us a mini-Eden[3] or micro-Paradise, a promised land, a sanctuary and its temple, a holy city. The mandala is a picture of our soul.

There have been many other ways of describing the soul-scape:

• to the Buddhists it is the boundless land, even "the pureland" where (said their leader) God is always at hand. . . .

• "the place of the heart" or "the heartspace" is an expression found in many cultures. . . . .

53

"I grew up in London during World War II, and—as you may know—the children were evacuated whenever possible to countryside homes so they'd be safe from the blitz. It was a hard time, but one of the joys for me and my brother was a special book. Before we were separated, my father gave us The Secret Garden and said, 'You may not always be able to go to school during the war, but take this book and study it carefully—and you will learn some important lessons.'

Naturally, that's a sure way to turn a kid off—we thought it would be boring and preachy, but it turned out to be a marvelous story of children who discover a walled-off garden that's been left untended. It's been there for years, but no one had paid it any attention.

Yes, we did learn a lot from the story, but most of all it left me with a longing for the secret garden that is part of me. Another version of this theme is The Selfish Giant, and also the Shangri-la tale, and the hidden cave of jeweled trees that Aladdin finds, and the castle of the Grail that Parsifal searches for—but I like the secret garden story best, because it's about the garden revealing its beauty gradually. And that's the way I've come to know the garden inside myself."

- in Tibet, the kingdom within is "the empire of greatest joy," because it is the abode of God. . . . .

- in the world of fantasy, stories like the Narnia tales of C. S. Lewis picture a world where time stands still; Narnia is a detailed analog of our own inner world, with its God-figure in the golden lion Aslan.

Each of these representations of inner home gives us a sense of harmony and balance; it is the mandala which is the consummate symbol of that ordered pattern. And at the core of the mandala, God:

"I am with you always."

Peaceable Kingdom, Garden of Love, Spring of Abundant Water

When people are asked what words or phrases come to mind in connection with

HOME,

three clusters of home-qualities seem to be most often expressed. (Did these emerge in your responses to the exercises of Chapter One?) They are:

1. *Peacefulness*—repose, sleep, rest, relaxation, comfort, security, not having to be 'on'
2. *Love*—unconditional acceptance, being able to be one's self, caring, listening, relationship, hugging, kissing
3. *Nourishment and Healing*—food, refreshment, oasis, renewal, licking wounds, being cared for, forgiveness, reconciliation

In the pages of the Bible, we find three special descriptions of the kingdom within that correspond to these three word clusters. These scriptural amplifications tell us even more about that place than do the mandalic biblical homes we've been considering: Paradise, promised land, the temple, the holy cities. The inner home has the same qualities as our ideal outer home.

Listen first to Isaiah on the sort of kingdom God has created for those who come home to their souls. He has already described life without a home, the life of the exile, then tells us that:

"There will be a highway in the desert called 'the road of holiness' . . . a road on which to travel home. The pilgrim will reach Jerusalem with gladness, and will be happy forever."

"The city will be shaded from the heat of day, and rain and storm . . . it will be a place of safety . . ."[4]

Then the prophet adds:

"The desert will rejoice and sing and shout for joy. . . . flowers will bloom in the wastelands. . . . every plant and tree in the land will grow large and beautiful. . . . the trees will raise their boughs and clap their hands. No fierce animals will pass that way. . . . the wolf shall dwell with the lamb, and the leopard shall lie down with the kid. . . ."[5]

A peaceable kingdom! There is a royal highway for each of us on which to travel to the inner home that has always been there. And it is our interior desert coming to bloom, our spiritual plant life growing large and beautiful, our own inner wolves who shall lie down with the lamb-like parts of ourselves when we finally come home.

This is not to say that the person who has committed to the life of the soul will know only tranquillity, for that is not true. Before those inner wolves lie down, they have to be confronted and tamed, and before the desert flowers will bloom we must also be pricked by their cactusy thorns. The peaceable kingdom Isaiah tells of is the end state, a glimpse of what is possible when we give the home within us—God's home—first place in our lives.

Home and the word 'love' are an obvious pairing, and we have a beautiful word-picture of how this second quality permeates our inner home in *The Song of Songs*, the famous love-poem of the bible. The anonymous author has picked up the enclosed paradisiacal garden image of Genesis. In a brief outpouring of passionate verse, which can be read at several levels, he gives us not only a celebration of human love (mirror of and teacher about divine love, its source) but also precious glimpses into the garden sanctuary inside each of us.

It is, primarily, a place of love—and not just calm, peaceful, down-home love, but also the sort of love that makes our heart leap for joy and our soul melt. *The Canticle of Canticles* is about yearning and longing for and languishing with love.

In the garden, it is spring: "the rains are over and done . . ." There is food and drink and plant life in abundance, a vineyard and even strong houses, with beams of cedar and rafters of cypress. The groom of the poem feeds among the lilies, in this place where one can be inebriated with love.

57

And yet, the garden-existence is punctuated with pain: the bride must search for the bridegroom, she must go forth into the fields where the flocks graze, among the rough shepherds. She has to venture out among those who strike and wound her and take away her veil. We too have to do this searching for the love-life in our own gardens. We will meet danger, have our illusions stripped from us on the inward journey . . . and, yet, it is worth the pain, the *Canticles* tell us—for the garden is a place where we are loved endlessly and always thought beautiful.

"If a man should give all for love, he shall count it as nothing," says the bridegroom, "for love is strong as death." And we, far removed from vineyards and pomegranates and cedars of Lebanon, hear these ancient words and cannot help but long for such a garden-experience of our own. It is available to all. The God of love lives at the core of the garden-like home within us . . . and waits for us to enter, move in, explore—and be loved in return.

"I was brought up with the idea of religion being really hard. You weren't any good unless you were suffering, and having fun was probably a sign that you were a terrible sinner. . . . at least, that was the message I picked up.

Thank God, there came a time in my life when I was sent a richer understanding of what it's all about. . . . although that didn't come until I was in my twenties. A friend next to me at work had this little quotation pinned up over her desk:

'To love God above all else involves three things:
> *warmth,*
>> *song,*
>>> *sweetness—*
and these cannot exist for long unless there is great quiet.'[6]

When I first saw this sign it was a mystery to me. It sure wasn't like anything I knew about loving God (my 'three things' would probably have been pain, self-denial and will-power). But I kept on noticing it, and I kept on noticing how my friend really was filled with warmth and song and sweetness—and, most of all, with love. She was living out the little quote over her typewriter.

Slowly, I have come to know the love of God and am even beginning to trust the feeling of being happy about that love. Wonderful!"

Kingdoms and gardens are static expressions of place, but the inner world is dynamic and alive, as well. The third quality most often associated with home is the idea of being nourished and healed—and for this, scripture gives us an image that flows: water, in abundant springs. Living water, the waters of life—we meet it in more than one place in the bible.

Jesus, speaking as the true son of a warm and sandy country, tells of the springs of living water, implying that the kingdom within is like a well or a fountain of holiness.[7] Water does not stand still, but bubbles up, gushes out, irrigates and cleanses and refreshes. It nourishes and heals. For all its permanence (like the peaceable kingdom) and its sense of enclosure (like the garden of love), our inner home is also alive and moving. (Life with God is never "either-or," always "both-and"; we will explore this thought further in chapters to come.)

So, for those of us who do respond to the call to seek first the kingdom of God, to take up residence in our inner home, we can expect the nourishment and healing of the living springs. Twenty centuries away from Jesus, we still hear him echoing the prophet's earlier invitation: "Come to the water, all ye who thirst."[8]

Who Will Dwell in the House of the Lord?

If the inner home is this beautiful, this exciting, we would think everyone would be eager to acknowledge it—but, as we have seen, this is not the case. There's one more scriptural picture that tells us about spiritual growth, and sheds light on why not everyone makes the inward journey.

The part of us that we don't know has been compared not only to springs of water, but also to the entire vast ocean: the first home, the mother of life. Out of the ocean, islands—or individual bits of consciousness—emerge as people develop, but most of our inner world stays hidden underwater, far from view. We are largely out of touch with (or completely unconscious of) this part of ourselves. Our souls remain uncharted territory filled with strange water life and sunken treasure which we never see, except for occasional signs of it which are washed up on the beaches of our own particular island.

The sea also hides from us the awareness that, underwater, we are connected to the other bits of land we can see from our own beachhead. These are other people; at our deepest level we all share in the same collective soul-layers. "No man—or woman—is an island . . . each is a part of the main . . ." is about the soul-world as well as the outer.

Let down your nets.

Jesus saying "let down your nets" can be heard as an invitation to go fishing in that deep sea to bring up the rich life that is there. The contents of the unconscious—like the fish and other creatures of the ocean—are plentiful, of wide variety, and life-sustaining. They are also elusive, easily slipping away; we need to learn fishing skills in order to catch them. Many among us do not have the patience to learn how to fish in these inner waters—or they give it a try, then find the task too time-consuming and attempt to take the inner fish by force. That doesn't work (in the holy land, during Jesus' time, real fish were caught only by nets, not spears or hooks, so the process would be as gentle as possible).

61

The next part of our book will give us details on the practical how-to's of "inner angling"—and even deep sea diving—drawn from the work of Carl Jung, who has been called "the Jacques Cousteau of the soul." Each sea-inhabitant brought to light lowers the water line around our personal island just a bit, increasing our amount of consciousness and also enabling us to see that we are connected to others.[9]

The riches of the sea shall be emptied out before you.

—Deutero-Isaiah

This helps us understand why so many aren't interested in the inner life: it is accessible only to those who both know of its existence and are willing to approach it on its own terms. The invitation to explore the depths—or, going back to our primary image, the invitation to acknowledge our inner home—is available to all, but many never hear it. "Many are called—but few show up!" Ours is not a culture where the interior life is greatly honored. It has been buried beneath an avalanche of external busyness and materialism. The words of Jesus

> to seek first the kingdom,
>   to come to the water,
>   to let down your nets,

are a gentle invitation, not a militant command. They easily get lost in our frenetic, fragmented lives.

So, it's as though the inner home which is available to all of us is way down the road for many. Their backs are turned to it; they don't even know it's there.

"You know, I realize there are people who seem a lot closer to God than I am—my wife is one of them, and I hate to admit it but my college son is another. But it's different for me. Look, I'm 44 and I have a good job as an accountant. They have time to read books and go to church if they want to—and my son has time to go off in the hills and commune with nature.

You know why they have that kind of time?—because I'm out working fifty-five hours a week to keep them in books and college monies. Oh, I believe in God, and I do get to church at Christmas. . . . but let's face it, stuff like 'exploring your soul' and 'searching for spiritual truth' is a luxury in this day and age. Someone's gotta pay the bills . . . and I got elected.

Maybe when I'm retired I'll have time for the inner world I hear them talking about, but I figure for now—as long as I don't do anything really wrong—I'm as close to God as I can be. My wife hears me say that and just looks at me with this Mona Lisa smile. I know she thinks it's a cop-out, but I love her for accepting me as I am and not trying to push her impractical interests on me."

People travel to wonder at the mountains, the sea, the stars and pass by themselves without wonderment.

—St. Augustine

A second group knows about the inner home from hearing or reading of it; they accept the inner reality intellectually but have little or no experience of it. They *know about* it—but don't *know* it. They're down the road a bit, a little closer to home. They've turned toward it just slightly (which is the meaning of the word *conversion*).

Even closer is a third group which has been touched by some experience that is decidedly spiritual: a time of love, God's hand in their lives, a dream they can't forget. This group is close enough to home to see its outlines, but (at this time) they're not homeward bound. There may be several reasons for their not taking the trip:

- an inner safety valve that says "I'm not strong enough" or "I'm just not ready"

- fears: of the unknown, of having to change, of what might be found in the dark, of evil they feel might be unleashed

- indifference or lukewarmness—or just laziness

- an activism that scorns introspection as "narcissism" or "navel-gazing"

- a life so busy they can't give up the time and energy which the commitment to the inner work demands.

Some of the people in each group will move down the road toward home at some time—and some will stay where they are, or go in the other direction, away from the inner kingdom. It is really vital that we respect the place where others are, and not promote our vision of spirituality as being right for anyone else. We just can't know about that.[10]

There is a fourth group of people: those who know they have no choice but to give themselves fixedly and singleheartedly to coming home

> to the peace of the kingdom,
>   the love of the garden,
>   the refreshment of the living water.

They learn very quickly that the inner realm is not always

> a paradise,
>   or a promised land,
>   or a temple,
>   or a holy city.

The road home also goes through wasteland and forest and desert and raging waters (Morton Kelsey refers to "the inner swamp"!), but—always—the God who is love waits for us at the heart of OUR INNER HOME.

Personal Journal Pages
The House in My Heart

Here is the cover of a book that was published in 1848.

THE OCTAGON HOUSE
A HOME FOR ALL
ORSON S. FOWLER

The author, who built a sixty-room octagonal house on the Hudson River in New York, gave details about a type of dwelling that had a short-lived popularity during Victorian times. After the crash of 1857, the fad for octagonal houses died out—for they were expensive to build—and, today, not many remain. The architects who favored octagon houses claimed to be building something "organic." It is outer home as mandala, just as the scriptural homes of this chapter are mandalic in form.

Here are some questions about this picture:

What would it be like to live in such a house? what would be the plusses? the minuses?

If I lived in a home that was a three-dimensional mandala, would it remind me of that unseen mandala, the one that is my inner home's pattern? or would that purpose be defeated because the pattern was so well-realized in wood and glass and brick? would the outer home become an end in itself?

Would life in such a home necessarily have the harmonious qualities of the mandala that speak of balance and integration? would the pattern affect those who dwelt therein?

Building my own ideal house: step one

If I could construct for myself an ideal home, what would it be like? Here are some details to consider:

style of house

floor plan

colors, decoration

areas for:
   daily living
   entertaining and relaxing
   work
   being alone
   storage

location

grounds

basement and attic

(This is a long project—a dream house takes a good while to build.)

Building my own ideal house: step two

Looking over my dream house, let me check out some important points:

have I included a place in which to pray, to meditate and recollect myself? what aids to reflection are there?

does my house have a "heart"—that is, a physical center?

in any way does the heart of my house say "God lives here"? (one way to do this is to have a home altar or prayer corner or shrine erected, either indoors or outside)

does my home feel like a holy place or sacred space at all? could I add this feeling to it? do I want to do that?

is my home in any way reminiscent of one or more of the images of home
we've been exploring? how?

        —enclosed garden
        —promised land
        —temple of God
        —holy city
        —peaceable kingdom
        —garden of love
        —spring of abundant water

is there any way I would like to remodel this home in my heart now that I've
thought about these questions?

what could I take from this idealized picture of a home and translate to the place in which I live now? are there some small ways in which I could make this dream home a reality?[11]

Owning My Own Home: a fantasy I can imagine some day when I have a half-hour or more of private time.

I go to the entrance to my ideal home that I have created. Before entering, I stand for a while looking over the outside. I may walk around the house, getting to know the grounds. I enter the house, and begin to explore it, taking as long as I need to enjoy and appreciate each room. I visit each room, and the attic and basement as well. When I feel I have spent as much time as I need to in my house, I leave, but not before promising myself to come back again, soon.

After taking this fantasy home tour, I can write down my reactions, especially noting the things which struck me most powerfully, what the surprises (if any) were, whether or not I met anyone in the house, and any changes I would like to make.

"One night I had a dream of a beautiful house I was supposed to build. I was astonished at how detailed the instructions were, with a floor plan half-drawn, and specific directions on the place in which I was to start: an inner chapel dedicated to Mary. There were twelve coves in the wall of this shrine-room, which was at the heart of the house, and each one was to be filled with a picture or statue of Mary that would show her in a different light.

Now, since I am a Catholic priest—and a long way from being a pastor or ever having a chance to build a real church, much less a home of my own—I knew the dream was about an inner house. It was such a powerful dream, and it indicated such a lot of work or active imagination, that I bought myself a special journal in which to put my house plans. And I didn't get my usual el-cheapo spiral pad, but bought a beautifully bound oversized book with parchment pages. This is the book I have begun about my house, and I pray over each piece of it before I draw it in. It's becoming an illuminated manuscript, just like those the monks used to make.

I began with the shrine room, just as the dream had said to. Slowly, different aspects of the feminine or of Mary have emerged, and I've sketched or written about them. The room is 12-sided, and all focuses not so much on Mary, but on Jesus. I've designed a small altar at the center of the room where, in my ideal home, I could reserve the Blessed Sacrament. The feminine figures surrounding God are ways that lead me to God; Mary works for me as an anima figure.

My design for the shrine room is almost finished, and I think the next part of the house that needs to be attended to is the outside. I sort of favor the native American southwestern pueblo look—white adobe against a bright blue sky, with dark wood for trim. I have the distinct feeling that I'm going to be working on this place the rest of my life!"

"When an image enters your heart
and establishes itself,
You flee in vain:
the image will remain with you."

*—the archangel Gabriel to Mary,
from a 13th century Persian poem.*[12]

Part Two

Homeward Bound

CHAPTER FOUR

The Long and Winding Road

Two Ways to Travel

I'm going home.

What memories that phrase stirs in everyone's heart, whether home be Dallas or Bay City or Dublin, Atlanta or Beirut or Johannesburg. We usually associate homecoming with outer home—but now we see it's about coming to our inner home as well.

For those who have responded to the call to come to the kingdom within—that is, to discover and live the spiritual life—there are maps and signposts for the journey. Just as there is more than one way to travel to an outer place, there is more than one way to come to the inner home. Let's look at the possibilities.

If you were planning a trip to South America, you could do it in a conventional way—that is, call a travel agent and book yourself on a tour of whatever countries you wanted to visit. The agent would make the hotel and transportation arrangements; all you'd have to do would be to show up when told and follow directions. Experienced guides would lead the way, point out the spots of interest, run interference for you if there were problems and, in general, shepherd you along. A good tour is a proven way to travel.

Another option you'd have would be to get some books from the library on South America, talk to people who had been there, plan your own itinerary and book your own arrangements, and then take the trip alone rather than as part of a group. This has advantages too.

A third possibility might be a combination of these two styles of travel: you might start out with the group and then take off on your own, perhaps rendezvousing with other travelers periodically.

In taking the journey to the home within us, we can also go as a member of a group, or make the trip a solo venture. There are precedents for both modes of travel.

I might make a commitment to a group that is about spiritual development—a church or other religious body, for instance, or a traditional American Indian tribe (if that is my heritage), or perhaps a school of spirituality such as yoga. With these, I usually have as plusses the accumulated wisdom and time-proven procedures of generations—or, if the group is newly-founded, at least I have traveling companions with similar ideals with whom to share the journey.

This way works, there is no question about it. The Christian churches, for instance, have been producing saints for almost twenty centuries now, and Judaism has a much longer track record of success, spiritually speaking. Yoga has been around for more than five thousand years, "yoking" (for that is what the word means) people to God. (The focus in the eastern practices is usually different from those of the west. We speak of the need for an "I-Thou" relationship with God, whereas yoga and other eastern disciplines speak of the annihilation of the ego, or the "I" part of us. However, in spite of differences in theology and psychology, the yogic *growth techniques* can fit into a western framework, as *Christian Yoga*[1] and similar books illustrate.)

The person who connects up with the time-tested groups that seek God will have many sure methods and much support available in his or her journey homeward. The pitfall of taking the inward journey *just* as a Catholic or a Sufi or a Methodist is that we may

completely identify with the group, and make group-think ours rather than allow for the individual ways in which God is also revealed. (And the *worst* of group spiritual sins is believing that there is only "one way" to God/heaven/happiness.) If our only means of spiritual growth are the precepts and practices of our faith or spiritual discipline, we may head for home very unconsciously— yet, for many, that is the way to travel (see note 7 for this chapter).

I can also decide to take the trip inward in a solo fashion, with little or no participation in any collective values. This is the path of the lone seeker: Thoreau off at Walden Pond or the person whose link to the inner world comes through the analytic process. Alone (or with just my spiritual guide), I will almost be forced to listen to the wisdom that is coming up from the God within me; I won't have the ready-made formulae of the institution to take the place of this individual listening. The pitfall in the solo trip, besides its loneliness, is that the pilgrim to the interior may negate age-old wisdom of the group that could be a great help and comfort, and be cut off from ritual, from devotional practices and sacramental life, and even from community.

Jesus gave us the advice to enter the kingdom through the narrow gate: that is, the gate only large enough for one to pass through. He recommends the path of the individual—the intentional exploring of our own particular soul-space. Yet, as a practicing Jew, and as source of a church with a sacramental life and ancient prayer forms and all the other group aids to spiritual growth, we know he believed in the value of the communal way as well.

In our time we have seen an exciting dialogue between the collective and the individual paths of spirituality, as the various psychologies that we call "transpersonal" (which means going beyond that which is personal, which is where the so-called "ego-psychologies" stay) have been cross-pollinating with organized religion. The very religious psychology of C. G. Jung, the famous Swiss thinker, especially has a tremendous amount to say to believers of all faiths. In it, the individual path is of primary importance—but Jung's insights can also illuminate the faith life we practice as members of organized bodies of religion. The two paths can integrate in a mutually supportive way (just as one might take the "combination trip" to South America). A blending of the time-honored guidelines of our faith and the lights that are particular just to ourselves gives us a rich pool of aids for our own inner alchemy.

The group and the individual avenues will, most often, support each other—although there may well come a time when the voice of the institution goes counter to the still, small voice within. In such times, which can be crossroads in our growth, the inner truth needs to be given primacy over the collective (a point on which most of the institutions themselves even agree).[2]

"When I was twenty-two I joined the Roman Catholic Church. Do you know what my number one reason for becoming a Catholic was?—well, it was because I thought I finally had found some place that had all the answers. 'Oh, great,' I thought, 'I'll never have to do any more of this wrestling with decisions that's been driving me bananas all my life.' ('Wrong reason for becoming a Catholic,' you say?)

Well, as I matured, what had looked like stability and Rock of Gilbraltar-type security became, instead, suffocating autocracy. I left the church for many years—now you're saying 'Wrong reason to leave the church,' right? Well, I'm a slow learner. . . .

Anyway, ten years more down the line I realized how much I missed the beautiful things about Catholicism: the Mass, the connection with its history, feeling part of the family that has produced so many colorful saints in the past, and is still doing so today, and—most of all—the Eucharist. I returned, and much to my surprise found out that the church isn't saying it has all the answers, but is asking lots of questions.

I'm glad I'm back—they don't speak of 'fallen-away Catholics' any more. The expression now is that you've been 'on sabbatical'! For sure, I won't and don't agree with everything I hear from the pulpit, but I know now that God gave me my own conscience to sort out the questions and answers for my life, and wants me to do the best I can, using the church as a wise teacher.

I've learned how to listen to God speaking with me every day, with the help of Sister Pauline, who's my spiritual director (she says friend is a better word than director: spiritual friend). It's all fitting together. Looks as though I finally got it right, doesn't it?"

So, two ways to travel: the entirely individual way and the plug-into-a-collective way. The individuation process (Jung's term for becoming the individual we were born to become) can happen through either path. But, as we've seen, the solo and the group paths are not exclusive. Rather, they're complementary, and we can blend them as we search for the buried treasure that is the kingdom of heaven, the home we have lost.

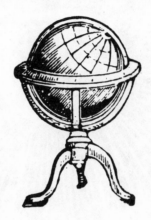

A Map for the Journey

The home we have lost? Were we there before?

When the first Christians, standing by the cross, heard Jesus' words about Paradise—the home to which he was going—they understood. Their tradition contained an earlier Paradise. The idea of Paradise *regained* is much more potent than the idea of Paradise the first time around.

And when the evangelist spoke and wrote of a new Jerusalem, those who heard him understood with special empathy; the hunger for a Jerusalem that would last was so compelling precisely because there had been an earlier Jerusalem—more than one, in fact.

The home which has been lost and which we have new hope of finding, is the most longed-for home of all.

So it is with us. We have seen how deeply the images of

HOME and COMING HOME

reach into us and resonate. They may stand for the house of our childhood, yes, but far more they stand for an inner home where we once lived.

"I've got this feeling that I guess you would call nostalgia. It's not for any place I ever lived, that's for sure, because I was brought up on the streets in Harlem. . . 'dragged up' would be a better way to say it, with no family life at all.

Well, there's this song by Neil Diamond that really gets to me. It's an old song, and he sings

'. . . . I've been this way before, and I'm sure to be this way again . . .'

When I hear it, I know the same thing is true for me. I can't explain it. I don't have the words for it—but it's as if things were once o.k. inside me, and if I just could find the secret, they'd be o.k. again. I'd feel some peace in my life.

In the song, he sings about

'. . . I've been released, and I've been regained. . . .' and how 'some people never see the light until the day they die.'

What's he singing about? I just know there was some place I once was in that was better—and I wish I could see the light before the day I die. Do you understand it?"

Many of us have this sort of spiritual déjà vu.

It's as though we once knew the peaceable kingdom,
had lived in the garden of love,
had tasted the spring of abundant water.
Well. . . . we did.

The map of spiritual growth or the individuation process which
C.G. Jung describes shows us how that can be. We have this
nostalgia for a lost inner home because we really did once live
there.

Jung's "map" starts with a description of the soul-state of the
very small child.[3] It is the Paradise state, for the tiny child is at
home with all the universe. Little children are with God, they do
live in the house of the Lord, who is "pleased to give them the
kingdom." It is a unitive state—a condition of union with the
creator and the created world—but it is not a *conscious* unitive life.
The infant has no objectivity with which to appreciate this way of
being. It is as though the child is at home—but does not know it.
He or she is pre-conscious, or naive.

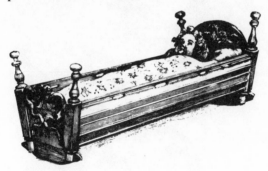

Within a few years of birth, the child has begun the task of
developing consciousness—that is, a sense of "I" or ego. With this
separateness or discrimination, the Paradise state is, gradually, left
behind. . . . and yet, for all of us it is part of our memories, hidden
away like some buried treasure.

The growing child begins to realize that he or she is apart from
everyone else and everything; he or she is unique, individual. And
we support this, of course: "God has called us each by name," we
relate, knowing that one needs a strong sense of self to make it in
the world. This "I" becomes the person's total identity, as he or she
forgets the "not-I" from which the ego had to separate, and there is

87

a stage of development where this egocentricity is appropriate. Our times have seen a great deal of attention paid to the ego, with books to help us believe that "I'm o.k." and "my own best friend." And it is vital for spiritual growth (or even just decent day-to-day functioning) that we like ourselves, feel strong.

Often, however, the task proves too difficult, and we go looking for a group that will take the place of that safe feeling we once knew (but have forgotten): the early home of our pre-and post-birth time. In the high school clique or the street gang, or the church which has all the answers, or the religious rule of life which defines our every move, or the movement or psychological school of thought that can become a cause, we find a safe nest. We slide back into a substitute womb, a collective which—if it accepts us—will be protection against the vulnerability of being alone.

Sometimes this need for safety is met through a partner "who will take care of me" (like Mommy or Daddy). It is usually a human partner—a spouse or a rescuer friend or a therapist or spiritual guide who makes us feel complete, but it can also be a divine partner. "God will take care of everything," we say; "give it to the Lord" (doing the right thing for the wrong reasons, reasons of dependency rather than mature relationship with God). Another way of protecting a fragile ego is by building a protective wall around ourselves. We may live out a prescribed role, such as "I am the mother of a family" or "I am a Lutheran minister," never asking if there is more to ourselves.

The person wrapped up in ego-needs feels that this "I" is the center of his or her being. In psychological terms, the ego is fixed or hardened in its rigid certainty that it is the center of all things, and in its defensiveness of this position.

The fairy tales tell us about this stage too: the person is sealed in a tower or turned to stone. Or, is covered over by animal skin (the frog prince) or feathers (the swan maiden) which hide his or her true nature. Or, the person is frozen by the Snow Queen. And always, in the stories, these unfortunates are "far from home."

The Scriptural language is equally telling: "heart of stone," "hardness of heart," even "idolatry" (at thinking the ego is the most important value of the person's life). The egocentric person is, truly, "in exile," as far from that original home as were the people of Israel from Jerusalem and the Promised Land.

Yet, that place where we once lived is still there. (A wonderful line from one of the original *Star Trek* episodes goes: "The cave"—meaning an earlier, primeval state—"is hidden deep in our memories.") It is alive in us, calling us back to it.

That sense of "there's more" which keeps resurfacing is the very thing most helpful in developing a healthy sense of self, the strong ego we need. All along the road we have clues that we are called to greatness, that we came from Paradise where we walked with God. The psyche is not neutral; it tends toward wholeness, not partiality. . . . and, so, all the time we are wrapped up in ego-needs, the God living at the core of our being is on the side of growth, calling us home, working in us:

"The kingdom of heaven is like a batch of yeast. . . . ."[4]

Once we ~~ha~~ve known God, we are ~~ne~~ver cured of God.

~~Fr~~ançois Mauriac

89

"When I was 50—can you believe it?—I finally *could* say I felt good about who I am. Boy, it sure took long enough! Now, I've gotten over being annoyed that it took so long, especially when I can see there are an awful lot of people who go through their whole lives never liking themselves or believing they're o.k.

Before I got to this point, I connected up to several groups which seemed to be where it was at:

- in the sixties, I was an aging hippie, just a bit too grown-up to be an acid-head or a flower child but still trying to make that scene and being happy that the local cool folks here in New York accepted me;

- a few years later, I had married and was into the country club set because my husband's business seemed to call for that. You can imagine: I needed a whole new wardrobe to go with the Connecticut countryside where we lived—sort of tweedy and golden retriever-y.

- then, because I thought I would crawl a wall if I played one more hand of bridge, I phased out of that group and became one of the dedicated volunteers at the church. Now, that was better, because I really felt I was accomplishing something, but I see now that a lot of my endless giving and always being available to paint scenery for the Christmas pageant and make cookies for the Sunday School parents' meeting came from my own need to be needed. That made me feel of value. I'm not putting myself down—that's just where I was.

And these were just the groups I hooked up with from thirty to fifty! I see now that I have been a living example of all four types of egocentricity I read about in a good book:[5]

- The Clinging Vine, *who is dependent on others, even addicted to them, living through them (this was me as Greenwich Village flake, and later as Supermom),*

- The Turtle, *who is in a protective shell to keep from being rejected, (this was me as Country Club wife—I never thought I really made the grade),*

- The Star, *trying to shine and get everyone's approval (me as Church Lady of the Year—and I can tell you, I was pooped after this wore off),*

- The Nero, *tyrannizing so that he or she can feel some power (well, this was me with my kids when they were little—I had 1001 rules, and a short fuse to go with them. That's exhausting too.)*

Anyway, I thank God I don't need to play these roles any more. Oh, sure, I still go to the club, and I want very much to help with my church, and I still have rules for my kids (like "keep your paws off my makeup"). . . . but I feel so different about myself now; I do these things because I want to, not because I have to. I don't look to other people to define who I am. I can truly tell you that I like that person I have become. Isn't that a good place to be?"

91

Lots of people never go beyond this second or egocentric stage of growth to the next. They will either remain insecure, forever searching outside themselves for the person or group who will complete them, reacting rather than acting—*or* they will finally feel good about themselves. . . . but not go beyond that stage of growth.

These people live and die without ever really returning to the home within, that place they once lived as very young children. But others will go home. They learn, usually very slowly, that the higher, larger life within (not the ego) can become the center of their personalities. A comparable cultural shift occurred when people moved from belief that the earth was the center of the universe to realization of the sun's centrality; geocentricity—or the immediate—gave way to far more expansive heliocentricity. The ego can be transcended (but needs to remain strong); it surrenders its primacy to that which is greater: God. This is what it means to return home—but, this time, consciously and with appreciation of this higher life within that is now seen to be our nucleus.

Jung's term for the image of that higher life was "the Self" (more correctly, "das Selbst" in the original German, the impersonal).[6] Believers of all faiths would speak more explicitly of God's presence within, adding religious language to Jung's psychological language.

With this reorganization of the personality around a new focal point, the so-called "ego-Self axis"[7] is established, so that there is a dialogue between the greater and the lesser parts of the personality. The religious language would be Martin Buber's phrase "the I-Thou dialogue," of which we spoke earlier. (This is why the eastern idea of getting rid of the ego won't work if we are using either Jung's map of growth or a strictly Jewish, Christian or

Islamic one. The "death to self" ideas of these faiths mean death only to the centrality of ME (the ego) as the ruler of the personality, "small 's' self" equalling ego in most psychological cryptology.)

As the transformation brought about by the change of heart or shifting of center continues, the unitive consciousness we once had begins to return. This time, we know what it is: we are at home with God, intimate with all of the created world, and aware of this state (which comes first, as the transcendentalists say, "in flashes of c.c."—cosmic consciousness—and then deepens and becomes our norm). It is what we had experienced as a small child, and what we have felt nostalgia for all these years—this time, however, we are not unconscious infants, but conscious adults who have made a choice to let this way of life become our highest value. We are ready to give up all else that this might be saved. We are home at last, after a long journey.

One gains by losing.

—Lao Tsu

I live,
now not I,
but Christ lives
in me.

—St. Paul

93

"All my life I've kept in shape. Now I'm 76, and a very young 76, if I do say so myself. There's life in this grandpa yet!

I jog by the lake every day, and I eat right. . . . no sugar or salt, lots of protein. I still shovel my own walk when it snows, which is a lot here in western Massachusetts.

However, I'll have to admit that my body's not what it was when I was 35. The signs of aging are there—but a good ten years later than most of the men I went to school with, I want you to know. My doctor tells me I've gotten almost an inch shorter, which I can hardly believe, and I can't chew corn off the cob or a good steak the way I used to. My hair's gotten thin, and even my deep barbershop baritone sounds more like a tenor today. By the way, did you ever hear My Gal Sal . . . ?

Our daughter Sarah has a baby boy, Gregory, and when I was playing with him the other day, it occurred to me that my body was taking on (just a little, mind you) childlike features like his—the thin hair and the weak gums and not being able to see very far. Then I remembered Jesus saying, "Become as little children."

Now, I know he was talking about spiritual childlikeness—and growing older I think I've gotten some of that too, for I just want to sit at his knee, so to speak—but now my body is paralleling my soul, if you know what I mean. It's a reminder of what's going on inside my heart.

Well, this makes the physical aging a little easier . . . not that you aren't going to catch me jogging on by twenty years from now. When you see that silver streak on the road . . . well, you'll know that's me!"

This, very simply, is the map of the journey homeward according to C. G. Jung's analytical psychology. Jung tended to speak of individuation as the last part of the journey, where the ego lets go of its central position in the psyche so that the greater Self might rule. Some of his followers speak of the entire process—leaving home and establishing a healthy sense of identity, then the giving over of me-centeredness as individuation, dividing it into these two parts.[8] Of course, the growth process is not this neat, but we can roughly diagram the three stages we've been discussing in this way:

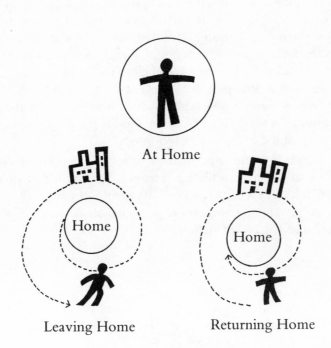

At Home

Home

Home

Leaving Home   Returning Home

And this is the story of the Prodigal Son, isn't it? He lived at home—but didn't appreciate it. Then he left to find out who he was (feeding pigs is a good way to learn). Finally he discovered that he needed to be at home—but this time by choice (which made all the difference). All the time, the father was home, praying and watching for the son's return—we might even say "calling him home" (and can we not add a yearning mother to the home front as well?).

—T.S. Eliot

"You Will Show Me the Path of Life"

What we've been examining is a "baptized" version of Jung's map for the inward journey; we have added the religious language that so easily overlays the psychological. Jung was writing as a scientist, for other scientists—so he intentionally tried to avoid speculation about religion. Even so, his work was thought too "mystical" by many of his colleagues; sixty years ago that word was a real put-down in the infant field of psychology. Today, with a half-century behind us, we rejoice at this marriage of science and faith.

Coming home to our inner sanctuary when we have a belief in God (whether or not we are members of some organized religion) is different from embarking on the journey without such a belief. This is the reason Jung was happy if someone who consulted him had an affiliation with one of the ancient faiths; he knew it could be a sure support to that person as he or she travelled home.

The *believer* doesn't just explore his or her psyche for the purpose of becoming "a total person"; when God is the picture, two big plusses are added to the inward journey:

The first: It becomes a pilgrimage of love. We have seen how the Lord lives at the core of the inner home. The monotheistic faiths of the west tell us of a God who calls us to an intimate love relationship, which is something far richer than "just" exploring the terrain of the world within.

My enemies surround me.

—King David

96

The second: The journey inward is not easy. It will be filled with pitfalls and moans and groans, as well as with joy. Knowing that the process is being guided by the God with whom "all things work unto good" is a great comfort; the faiths which make some sense of suffering will give the seeker a support that the world of psychology, alone, cannot.

In several places in his *Collected Works*, Jung speaks of the "circumambulation of the Self," as though the journey homeward were a spiral and the center a magnet, drawing the parts of the journeyer into a crystal-like formation. (The crystal, like the mandala, is a perfectly balanced construction.)[10] Jung speaks of the Self *yearning* for reconciliation with the ego; religious language would say that the love of the indwelling God calls us back home.

Jung also has a most interesting way of speaking of the ego: it runs "round this central point like a shy animal," he says, "at once fascinated and frightened, always in flight, and yet steadily drawing nearer."[11] As this process continues and we come ever closer to the lost and now-found-again home, the qualities of the center grow clearer and clearer.

Throughout scripture we have examples of this same spiral path:

- We have seen how the bible begins with a home, the garden, and ends with a new (yet very like the old) home, heaven.

- The story of the people of Israel traces the same pattern: they have a home, the promised land from which they must go into exile and become slaves ("captive Israel"), and they return to it ("ransomed Israel"). First they leave for Egypt, then for Babylon. In our time we have seen homeless Jews return once again to their native land, with the creation of present-day Israel. One of the things that made this possible is the strong sense of identity the Jewish people have maintained over the centuries: it is the group or collective equivalent of the strong individual ego that is necessary for our regaining of home.

- Jesus' story also has this same kind of leaving and returning. His parents make a round trip from their home in Nazareth, to Bethlehem, then back to Nazareth (via Egypt, according to one of the infancy narratives). Jesus also comes from a heavenly home, and at the end of his time here, returns to it. . . . returns to prepare a place for those who will follow him to an eternal home.

. . . the secret sits in the middle and knows . . .

—*Robert Frost*

97

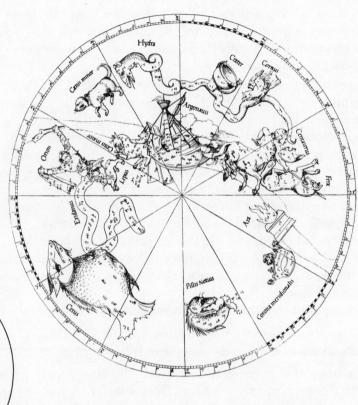

> *For it is in dying that we are born again.*
>
> —St. Francis

And look how the voyage of the moon-landers, which we spoke of earlier, is also a living out (or flying out) of this spiral map of the inner journey. Their actual flight away from Earth *was* a spiral, landing them in a place as bleak and barren as any scriptural wasteland. And it was the gravity of the Earth—the home that had always been there while they were gone—that actually pulled them back as they retraced their spiral course.

The spiral map is, simply, the story of one way of living that must die so that something better can be born, which in turn must die so that an even finer new creation can come about. It is a picture of the paschal mystery—and within each stage of the map we are constantly being "born again" as we outgrow or "let die" old ways of being. The conversion process continues all our lives.

". . . (After Vatican II) theologians began to speak of grace at work 'anonymously' in the hearts of all women and men . . . there is only one vocation for all . . .: 'conversion,' should it occur, would feel like coming home."

commentary on The Church in the Modern World,
in a National Catholic Reporter editorial,
February 8, 1985.

We can't travel on the path to home using this or any map in a lock-step fashion. Spiritual growth isn't a game of snakes and ladders. (Robert Johnson says that rearrangement of the personality is like taking two steps backward and one step forward—but then you find out you were going the wrong way all the time, so it comes out all right!)

Our drawing closer and closer to the kingdom is God's work, not our own. However, there are things we can do to facilitate the process and cooperate with grace, and we will look at these next. They will help us be able to say, some day:

"I was asleep, but now am awake"

"I was blind, but now I see"

"I was lame, but now I leap like a stag!"

"I was deaf, but now I hear"

"my tongue was dumb, but now I sing"

"I was hungry, but now am filled"

"I was captive, but now am set free"

"I was broken-hearted, but now am healed"

"I was thirsty, but now am refreshed"

"my knees were weak, but are now made firm"

"I was afraid, but am now made strong"

"I was dead, but now am alive"

And, best of all,

"I was in exile. . . . but now have come home."

99

Personal Journal Pages
Getting Ready for the Trip

When preparing for a journey it's usual to make arrangements in advance. Here is a checklist of preparations for the inner journey (this is also helpful for those who are already launched on inner travels).

1. *Gather supplies*:

- a journal

- writing tools (colored marking pens or crayons are a big help)

- a dream log

- books—a basic list:[12]

The Bible (Old and New Testaments)
by John Sanford—*The Kingdom Within*, *The Invisible Partners* and *King Saul: The Tragic Hero* (Especially Appendix A) (Paulist Press)
by Morton Kelsey—*Dreams: A Way To Listen to God* (Paulist), *Adventure Inward* (Augsburg) and *Christo-Psychology* (Crossroad)
by Carl Gustav Jung—*Man and His Symbols* (large color edition, Doubleday), *Psychological Reflections* (an anthology, Jacobi and Hull ed., Princeton University Press)
by Robert Johnson—*He, She, We* (Harper and Row)

2. *Set aside time*:

What amount of time do I have for the inner work?

How can I clear more time—quality time? What can I let go of?

How must my priorities be rearranged in order to put the search for God at or near the top of my list?

Do I have some way to help me sanctify the days of my life? that is, do I follow the liturgical year? or keep in touch with the ebb and flow of the seasons (or even the moon)?

3. *Space/Place*:

Do I have a place for prayer and reflection, for journal-writing and study?

If not, could I create such a place?

What could I put in such a place that would help me use it well? (suggestions: comfortable chair, good light, cross and/or pictures that are evocative, table for supplies and books; if the place is not where I live—my car, a corner of a church, for example—what could I keep in one bag or briefcase to carry with me?)

4. *Traveling Companion(s)*:

Do I have one fellow pilgrim with whom I can share the journey?

Is there a trained guide I can visit regularly? or occasionally?

Is there a support group of other people who are also doing this inner work with whom I can share and learn?

5. *Readiness*:

Are there ways I could improve my health, so that the physical vessel for my soul will be as much of a help as possible in my travels?

What fears do I have about the inner journey? Can I get these down on paper so I can begin to look at them?

Are there goodbyes I need to say—to other projects or commitments, to people (temporarily or even permanently), to habits?

6. *Resources*:

Do I have "sufficient funds"—that is, am I able to make a commitment of energy to the inner work? Or are my energies scattered in so many directions that I could not pursue the inward path with sustained focus and single-heartedness?

Here is the reply of an experienced spiritual director to the questions:
What is the biggest handicap people face in growing spiritually? Is there any one thing that most holds people back?

"That's an easy question to answer. The one biggest hindrance I find is one I also struggle with in my own life . . . and that is the inability of so many of us to give the spiritual life the prime time and energy it deserves. It's as though we say, 'Oh, of course, I want to seek first the kingdom of God—but I don't want to have to give up anything else in order to do it.' Actually, we don't behave that consciously—for if we did, we'd hear ourselves and know that what we were saying didn't compute.

Let me give you an example: Jack Smith comes to see me and asks if I'll be his spiritual companion or guide. I say, 'Let's give it a try for a while, and see how it goes. By the way, Jack, what kind of spiritual practices do you find most helpful? What sort of things are you doing already?' He'll usually speak of prayer and community worship, often some spiritual or growth-oriented reading.

'That's fine, Jack,' I say. 'How would you feel about adding a couple of practices to those you've already adopted? For instance, what is the best time of the day for you? And could you make that your special prayer time? Also, I would like you to keep some sort of log of how you feel God is being revealed to you each day— it doesn't have to be extensive; just a few lines in a notebook will be fine. How does that sound?' Jack will agree to try these two things, but when we meet again, he'll often say he was too busy with his work or his family to follow up. I would then suggest some other practice, such as logging his dreams (if he's open to that) or using the daily scripture readings as part of his prayer. And again, the report will often be 'I just didn't have time.'

At this point, I will usually confront Jack about his seriousness to advance spir-itually—I'd never want to dismiss someone lightly, of course. He's there by the grace of God, knowing that he wants more of the inner life. I often ask someone like Jack to draw a chart of concentric circles, and put the priorities of his life in them, starting with the most im-portant at the center, and work-ing outward.

I hope he will come to see that the most important thing (which he will almost always write down as 'relationship with God') deserves his best time and en-ergy—the first fruits, if you like. And that often requires some real life changes, even major changes. . . . reprioritizing for better stewardship can be very scary.

When you read the reports of spirituality even fifty years ago, or less, it seems the biggest pitfall was that directees would lean towards going overboard—re-member all the stories about long hours of prayer and fasting, with people fainting away? Occasionally, some do come who are so wrapped up in their own inner life they're letting the outer be neglected, and I remember once a young mother who had decided to discipline herself by wearing a rough metal belt under her clothes—but over-zealousness doesn't seem to be today's curse. If anything, the outer world is too much with us, and we've gone to the outer extreme of not giving the inner world equal time. To become more holy, we have to make choices, often setting aside other very good things—perhaps keeping fully abreast of the news, or even volunteer work we've been doing, or seeing friends as often as before. If one is not to be just a dilettante, a spiritual dabbler, there will always be choices between good things that call on our energy and the best thing—being with the Lord. If we just give left-over time to God, not much growth will occur. The good can be the enemy of the best, you know.

Believe me, this is a struggle for me too! I can't tell you how much I've learned from the people who come to me. They're an inspiration!"

What is my reaction to this opinion? Does it apply to me in any way?

CHAPTER FIVE

How Do We Come Home?

Searchers for Hidden Treasure

"The kingdom of heaven is like a treasure buried in a field." That makes those who would come home to the kingdom not only pilgrims (and fishers in the deep), but also

Seek and you shall find.

- treasure hunters, following our maps and being willing even to risk our lives that the precious hidden riches might be found;[1]

- inner archaeologists, patiently sifting through layers that cover other worlds, bringing the lost things to light;

- miners of precious metals and stones, working slowly and carefully to chip away encrustations that hide the precious veins and gems in the darkness;

- cave-explorers (spelunkers, to be precise), who venture into hidden inner spaces that often contain incredible beauty—as well as knowledge.

These are risky occupations, but at the same time they have about them an aura of excitement: the precious discovery may be just around the corner! One of the most delightful Grimm's fairy tales captures the same fascination about searching for the hidden:

The Twelve Dancing Princesses

Once upon a time there was a king who had twelve beautiful daughters. Every night, after everyone in the court had fallen asleep, the princesses would put on their finest party clothes and slip down a secret staircase, which was connected to their room by a hidden door. Down they would go, into a subterranean world which lay beneath the palace—and which no one knew about but themselves.

In the hidden world which was their nightly destination there was a park filled with trees bearing leaves of silver and gold and diamonds. And there was a great lake, which the princesses crossed in twelve boats guided by twelve handsome princes. They were taken to a beautiful castle, from which they could hear the merry music of horns and trumpets.

The princesses danced all night, each with her prince, until three in the morning. By then, they had worn holes through their dancing slippers and so had to be taken home again, retracing their route. By dawn, they were back in their beds sleeping soundly, their shoes by their bedsides.

Their father, the king, was very perturbed by his daughters' inability to be present to court life during the daylight hours, and so he offered the hand of any one of the princesses to whoever could discover the reason for their fatigue—and the holes in their slippers. Many fine young men tried to solve the mystery and failed, until finally a soldier passing by took up the challenge. With the aid of an invisible cloak which enabled him to follow the girls on their nightly journey to the nether world, he discovered their secret and won a princess for his bride.

The original story goes into much more detail, and is usually told from the perspective of the soldier (who is, sometimes, a young gardener). It is found throughout central Europe and the British Isles in over one hundred variations;[2] as with any story handed down and retold over and over, we see that it has remained popular because—in some way—it is our story too.

This fairy tale is about that part of us that is willing to risk going down into the dark, hidden world we cannot see—the unconscious part of the psyche or soul—in order to explore its unknown potentialities. And that part of us, the story says, is *twelve-fold*—twelve-sidedness being symbolic language for "containing all possibilities," like the twelve months of the year or the dozen signs of the zodiac or the twelve apostles.[3] It is a young, adventurous part of ourselves, the story says, and a feminine part; in the language of analytical psychology the feminine is the principle in us which unites our separate parts into a whole (like the mandala).

And, best of all, the exploring-princesses' part of each man and woman (for we all have such a part) is child of a king! It is a royal part of ourselves, heir to a kingdom . . . if we can but discover it. The treasure of richer life for which the princesses search is not found in the extraverted daytime world of their outer home; the story tells us we must get to know another equally valid reality, one to which many of the people around us are asleep.

The entrance to this other world with its interior castle is found in the most quiet space available to the princesses, their bedchamber. The inner world is not reached by some busy kitchen-like or office-like part of ourselves, but through our most quiet place—the place of prayer and reflection. And to visit it, we need "party clothes" and "dancing slippers"; the visit to the world within is cause for celebration. Joining in the dance, in fact, has long been a metaphor for living in a religious way.

The hidden inner kingdom of the princesses is across the lake; they have to put out onto the water to reach it, just as the apostles had to do in order to let down their nets. All these images can be taken as exterior signs about outer water and boats, but they are also images of our soul-scape and the ways to explore it.

Finally, we see that the princesses spend *so much* energy in the hidden realm that they wear out their shoes! They have no standpoint left with which to take their place in the outer world, which is why the story has to end with them being rescued from their one-sided adaptation. (Most of us have the opposite problem: too much caught-upness in *external* reality.) We don't know from the story if they were able to find the necessary balance between inner and outer; in the language of psychology we would say there must be a dialogue between consciousness and the unconscious. They were in the not-uncommon position of giving the contents of the unconscious *too much* credence, a pitfall many of us fall into when we first discover the power of the inner world.[4] Again, we see that the "both-and" approach is superior to the "either-or" dichotomy, in the spiritual life as well as elsewhere. We can hope the king did not seal up the hidden door to the underworld and that the princesses' visits to it continued.

We can cultivate the searching-princesses' side of ourselves, becoming inner space explorers. We can become spiritual detectives, seekers-out of clues about the path to the inner home that is our own most precious hidden treasure.

Show me the way to go home.

One way to view the spiritual journey is to see God as the "master teacher" living within us, longing for union with us, calling us home. The curriculum for our homecoming is already prepared—not in a predestined sense, but because God is outside of our time, and therefore knows the possible future as well as the past and present. So, our task is to first allow the clues about the homecoming process to become conscious, and then to use them. The good spiritual detective will become fine-tuned, able to see the many hints we are sent daily; these are our God's present-day form of revelation (with a small "r"). We learn to *expect* them. The theological "principle of mediation" says that God acts upon us and is available to us through secondary causes; these are our clues.

What kind of clues about the inner odyssey are there? We might divide them into things that bubble up from the interior:

- moods and feelings, especially the powerful ones that say, "Pay attention!"

- dreams—"visions of the night" or spontaneous daytime fantasies—which we can learn to capture in our "dream nets" and carry with us so they will release their meaning

- memories that surface ("Why am I reminded of this long past event just now? what does it say to me today?")

- prayer experiences, experiences of God—ones that we prepare for and others that are just pure gifts

- physical changes (which often have psychospiritual contributors)

- unexpected behavior on our part: we find ourselves saying or doing things that leave us feeling "That's not like me at all! Where did that come from?"

111

- journal entries: we may set out to record something and find more information surfacing than we expected; also, by re-reading our journal, we will see overall patterns not discerned at the time of writing.

You have eye. but do not see

And, a complementary category, clues that come from without ourselves:

- the people who attract or repel us; we meet parts of ourselves in projected form

- everyday events—sometimes involving other people and sometimes not, sometimes pleasant and sometimes not—about which we can ask, "Why is this happening to me now?"

- changes in our tastes or needs or way of living: clothing, friends, hobbies, how we spend our time, things we collect, our choice of entertainment, our enthusiasms, a felt need for therapy or spiritual direction. All are barometers of the climate of our soul.

- words and phrases and images and stories that reach out and touch us especially; from television, from scripture readings or hymns, from the movies, from newspapers and magazines and books, from other people

Thank you, Lord, for sending that rotten person into my life this morning—I'd really like to punch him in the nose, but I know there's a reason he's here right now. . . and that you are helping me learn yet one more thing about myself. Please keep me from breaking his neck—and, as I said before, thanks a lot. . . . I think. . . . Amen (and please don't do it again).

- synchronistic events: those unexpected "coincidences" that cannot be understood in terms of cause and effect.[5]

   These are the tiny clues in the treasure hunt for the kingdom within. They will usually be sent in clusters, to make sure we get the message. We can learn to see them as such, and thank the God who sends them.

   Good detective work involves piecing together seemingly unrelated scraps and findings until, at last, sense begins to emerge out of mystery. We need to trust that even though we don't always see the overall plan, the Sender of clues has it in mind; eventually, most of the bits and pieces will be understood and fit into a total picture. As the journey progresses, we begin to appreciate how this is so—but at the beginning of the pilgrimage home the things we are learning can seem very hit or miss. (Isn't this how the Israelites wandering in the desert must have felt? It was only long after they had entered the promised land that they were able to look back and retell their history and mythologize it, seeing the larger pattern God had described for them. Then, and only then, did the details fit; while they were living them out, all they had was their often-wavering trust in their God.)

   C. G. Jung tells us about the treasure hunts of the medieval alchemists, whose efforts to make gold out of some *prima materia* he recognized as a parallel to our spiritual explorings:

> "(The alchemists spoke of) the 'treasure hard to attain' . . . whose presence was suspected in the dark . . . *massa confusa*" (or chaos). "Our understanding," they would say, "aided by the 'celestial and glowing spirit', ...transforms this natural work of art . . . so that 'our heaven' may come into reality."[6]

The treasure, they thought, was already contained in the confusion of the alchemical elements; our hidden treasure is already behind the unordered fragments of our lives. And, going back to the world of fairy tales once more, we can recall how the treasure that would mark the end of a journey was *always* hard to find: the pot of gold at the end of the rainbow, the golden ring in a river bed or a troll's hutch, the bluebird of happiness.

"As an old time Hardy Boy fan, it made me very happy to learn that Carl Jung, from whose work I've learned so much, was an avid reader of detective stories—English thrillers were his favorites.

And he spoke of how the inner guides sent in dreams are modern-day versions of Mercurius, the alchemical guide or psychopomp[7]—what a great word! It means the one who conducts a solemn procession through the psyche. Mercury in modern dress is the detective, who can be seen as our best present-day image of one who searches in the dark and uncovers clues. The alchemists thought their work was sacred work . . . and surely, what we are doing as we deliberately explore our souls is even more sacred.

I know there have been times I've pictured myself as sort of an interior Charlie Chan (although sometimes it's probably closer to Inspector Clouseau!). Now I understand better why I've always loved detective yarns. It's elementary, my dear Watson!"

The tracking-down instinct lies deep within us: think how often we use our detective skills in non-spiritual pursuits: "I must have that last piece of depression glass to complete my set," "I've searched all over for the right dress for the prom," "Finally, I've completed my collection of pipes (or fishing lures or mounted boars' heads or beer cans or matchbook covers or. . . .)—what can I collect now?" Long ago, Jesus had talked about hunting for and finding the missing piece: a lost sheep, a lost coin. And one of the most lasting Christian legends is about the long search for the Holy Grail, the chalice of the Last Supper. The impetus to search for that which is lost or hidden is inborn in us. We employ it outwardly in quests as simple as those for the missing puzzle piece or crossword answer, and as complicated as the search for a home of our own; at its finest it is introverted and utilized in the mystery that is soul-making.

The detective is a double image: he or she is, first, a listener, a watcher for clues, a ponderer . . . exemplifying the receptive (or feminine) principle, which we all have. (In ancient China, the spiritual seeker was compared to a cat watching a mousehole.)

But the detective is also the person of action. Once the clues are gathered, the detective records them and reacts to them, and then acts on the knowledge they have revealed. This doing-ness is the active (or masculine) principle in action; each of us has this capacity as well.

The detective combines both receiving and carrying out, rather than living just one or the other modality. As we become sleuths of the spirit, we can find the hidden treasure of the kingdom of God in both these ways. It's really *homework* we're doing—our search is leading us home.

"I had a dream that made a tremendous impression on me. I call it The Hidden Stairs.

I am visiting an empty apartment building, and go up to the second floor to see if there is a place I can claim for my own. It is raining outside, and the air in the building is very close and damp.

The second floor apartment is pleasant, however. I would like to stay here so I can be alone sometimes. I go to the back door of this apartment and find it opens onto a hall, and has an extra, more private room across from it. I go into this room. It is very small.

It has another door, which I open. I find it leads to a back flight of stairs which go down to the first floor and below. I see an old woman in a long white dress (just like the one I am wearing) at the foot of the stairs. It is very dark down there, and she can't see me yet. I stand perfectly still. Then she begins to come up the staircase. I am frightened and cannot move. Time seems to have been suspended.

I felt as if this dream was an invitation for me to take more time and space for myself. The house has so many unexplored areas; maybe I have found a place where I can breathe more easily. In the dream I cross a threshold. I go on to explore more of the empty house. The old woman must have some connection to me, as we are wearing identical nightgown-like dresses. Maybe she is the woman I will grow into some day. At any rate, I certainly can't avoid her and she isn't the least bit frightened of me. I have no choice but to meet her and see what it is she wants of me.

Here is a picture I drew of this dream . . ."

116

Tools and Skills for the Journey

Just as good detectives have their magnifying glass (at least, in popular fiction), their fingerprint dusting powder and an assortment of other aids, so too there are tools and skills for spiritual development. Most are widely known: prayer, making scripture our own, living in harmony with the seasons—both liturgical and natural. Some others have been around quietly for centuries, and are having a well-deserved renaissance in our time: attention to one's dreams, journal-keeping, care of the body as a spiritual practice.

At the end of this chapter, there is a checklist of the many ingredients of the spiritual life. Here, we want to focus on those skills which are most representative of the uniting of Jung's psychology and our Judaeo-Christian heritage, for that is the point of view of this book. The overall principle they illustrate is that there needs to be a continuing dialogue between our consciousness and that in us which is unconscious. We learn about the unconscious parts of ourselves by the clues that are sent, the inner and outer clues listed earlier in this chapter. As we get to know these not-yet-revealed aspects of the soul, they become conscious—temporarily, if we don't do our work thoroughly, or permanently, if we do. When we really get to know that which is now unknown—or below the water line—

we lower the water line, gaining more consciousness for ourselves.

(Another way to say this is that we try to live a life of awareness of the inner home and the God-center of that home; this is the practice of the presence of God about which the great mystics tell us—and Jung's understanding of *how* we can do that gives us skills in addition to the traditional religious ones of prayer and sacramental life and spiritual reading and self-discipline.)

Let's focus on six special keys to the inner dialogue:

- one is the major way in which the unconscious lets itself be known: *our dreams*

- the next two are about encouraging the contents of the unconscious to release their meaning, so we can make them our own: *active imagination* and *living with images*

- the fourth and fifth are about ways of grounding and containing what we learn, by putting it "out there" and thus getting a more objective look at it, . . . so that our gifts from the sea will *stay* with us: *keeping a journal* and *sharing with a spiritual friend*

- and the final key is a special extra: *finding ourselves in favorite stories*

Let's take a short look at each of these six powerful ways of growth, from the specific point of view of homecoming.

Our Dreams

Learning the language of dreams is like learning a foreign language—a forgotten language, as it is often called. And the best way to learn French or Chinese or dream-ese is just to get in there and listen to it. Books help. There are wonderful books today on dreaming within the context of one's faith;[8] we have reclaimed this biblical way of listening to God and gone way beyond pop dream books that have a ready answer as to the meaning of each and every symbol.

A dream log with pen or pencil ready has become a standard fixture in bedrooms across the country and around the world. The best dream recall seems to come to those who faithfully record every dream fragment, unedited, even numbering and dating these visions of the night (or bits and pieces of them).

Once the dream is caught in the dreamer's net (or log), the images in it can be listed; associations for them will come forth

("the house was like my grandmother's house"); images will also
remind us of similar scenes or people or things from folklore and
mythology and today's stories. We can do some sort of active
imagination (see below) with a dream image, then listen to what
the dream is saying as though it were a play or a movie or a
scripture story whose theme we were summarizing.

   We cannot work with each and every dream, but will know the
important ones by the impact they make on us at the level of
feeling. With those we will try to discern what the dream message
is. What does the God-author of this dream want to let me know
that I don't already know? (for dreams are compensatory—that is,
they don't rehash events of our waking life but inform us of things
the conscious mind does not yet know, often using daily
happenings and familiar faces).

   When we have lived with a dream for a while it will usually
release its meaning; the awareness of what a dream has to say to us
is often called the "click" experience—an inner sureness. And we
will also want to make some sort of response to that message, a
response that goes beyond just the intellectual understanding we
have of the dream. What can I do to keep this new learning about
myself alive? How best can I honor the dream that has been sent to
me? These are the sort of questions that will lead us to the right
response.

The subject of dreaming is at once tremendously complex, filling volumes, and at the same time extraordinarily simple. In terms of the spiral map of growth we looked at in the last chapter, the dreams can be seen as messages coming from the core of our being, that firm center or home base where God lives in us. And they are sent, according to this way of viewing spiritual growth, to help us understand what we must do to move along in our soul-journey, no matter which part of it we are on. Readers for whom this spiritual approach to dreaming is new will want to read one or more of the valuable books referred to in the notes for this chapter, and may also find helpful the "6 Steps for Honoring Your Dreams" at the end of this chapter.

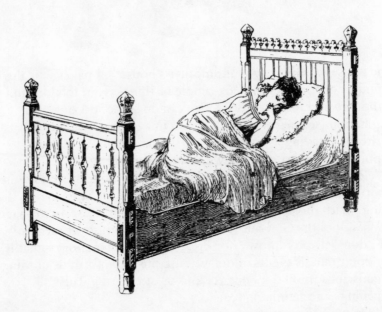

"God speaks to us in dreams and visions of the night," says scripture. And we listen—whether with intent to understand in detail, or just to appreciate the wealth of the inner sanctuary from whence cometh the dream. Like the twelve princesses, nightly we can cross into the other world. This is a sacred task. We are listening to our Creator . . . creating.

"Last year when I was twelve, my Mom gave me a folder of pictures she had saved for years. They were drawings she and I had made of my dreams. Every morning from as long ago as I can remember there would be paper and crayons on the table at breakfast time. When I was really little, my Mom used to ask me to tell her about my dreams—and she would draw a picture of what I told her, and write the words I said under it.

Later I would do this too, until I started school anyway—then I was too busy, except on weekends and in the summer. I never knew she had saved all these pictures, but she did, and she saved my sister's too. I found some about a tiger that used to chase me around at night when I was maybe four or five, and I found some about wanting to fly airplanes when I got bigger. They're really special—I'm glad she's saved them all these years. My parents are into what dreams mean and all that stuff, but for me my dream pictures are more a record of how much there is inside me, how rich I am in there. That makes me feel good."

Active Imagination

Listening with consciousness to the as-yet-unrevealed parts of ourself is one thing; doing something with what we have heard is another. Jung used the phrase "active imagination" to describe the moving of the unconscious contents into a space and place where they can be assimilated into our conscious attitude.

When we are sent one of the clues that tells us something about our spiritual growth—an inner clue, like a dream, or an outer clue like a strong feeling toward a person in our life—we can do something with it. The conscious part of ourselves, our ego, can engage this clue about unknown contents of the psyche in a variety of ways, so that it will begin to give up its meaning.

Again, the subject of active imagination has been written about at length by today's spiritual masters, and the reader is referred to the footnoted books for details on active imagination, as well as to the section entitled "Active Imagination" at the end of this chapter.[9] For our purposes now, let's take just a few lines to explore briefly three of the most effective styles of active imagination.

Imagine that you have recently bumped into a slapstick clown in more than one place in your life: perhaps you dreamt of him, then saw a clown on television who was just magnetic for you, then received a call from a friend with a surprise invitation to the circus—where, of course, you would see more clowns. By this time, the point is beginning to sink in: "Pay attention to clowns!" Your response might be, "Fine—but how do I do that?" You might:

1. Converse with clown-ness, especially any inner sense of clown in yourself. This can be done in your imagination, silently, or a conversation can be spoken (when no one's around to hear and wonder just when you came unglued); better still, a conversation with "essence of clown" can be written down or taped and might develop along these lines:

Myself—Clown-ness, you keep appearing in my life. What are you about?
Clown—Oh, come on—everyone knows what a clown's about . . .
Myself—Well, yes, clowns are supposed to amuse and make us laugh. But I'm asking why you're coming to me in so many ways all of a sudden.

Clown—Maybe I want you to laugh a little more.

Myself—Is that it? Am I so serious? But there's more to you than that—I sense you're the traditional sad clown hiding behind a happy face. Are you sad? Are you about some part of me that won't admit I'm sad?

(and so on)

When we allow ourselves to get in a prayerful and quieted state before beginning such a dialogue, the things the clown (tiger, old women, young child, ocean, rock. . .) within us will say are amazing. Our ego really can get out of the way and allow the inner contents to speak—and they have much to say, for we usually have been ignoring them for some time.

2. We can allow the image we are bringing to consciousness to move inside us; we might feel and act like a clown, for instance. There are lots of times in our everyday routine to work in such experiences, such as driving the car or walking to work or doing the dishes. (Of course, in these instances you would want to keep your inner clown under some restraint. However, you might be able to find a clown troupe to join, in which case the clown within can have full play.)

At the very least, we can allow an inner figure to have its life in us for a short time, even if it's just in spurts of walking upstairs as he or she or it would, or moving across a room in the way native to this inhabitant of the unconscious.

3. Sketching or painting an inner image, or sculpting it in clay, or finding a picture which is like it in a magazine and posting that where it will be seen, or drawing an image in the sand or dirt— these are some of the art-related styles of active imagination, and they are *very* helpful. One reason they are so valuable is because they use the pre-verbal language of picture rather than words; they use right-brain language, the language of the child—remember, it was the child who was once at home in the pre-conscious state . . . and it is by becoming like a little child in many ways, that we will return to that home consciously.

When we engage an inner image in one or more of these ways of active imagination, we feel we have befriended it—and it in turn stays around as our friend, or at least as a known sparring partner.

Our overall guideline is to continue the dialogue between consciousness and the unconscious so that we may have *more* consciousness; as the inner contents become known to us they move from under the water line to that island above it. And, if we keep attending to them, they can even stay there.

There is a valuable second way the active imagination techniques can help us keep the dialogue alive. There are dry times, when we seem to be getting *no* clues. The place where God lives within us seems like a dream, a beautiful idea that vanished with the dawn. We think things like, "How foolish I was to imagine I was supposed to do all this inner work—that's for saints, for special people . . . my world is just the daily rat race." It is then that we use active imagination to stir things up inside, to reopen the channel. In such times it is our consciousness that has to initiate the dialogue, rather than the unconscious with its clues. Some ways we might do this are:

- go back to a special dream or experience that connected us with God; re-dream or re-experience it, live it again.

- dialogue with the empty, dry, desert-like feeling itself ("Why are you here?", "Where did you come from?", "What can I do for you?"). We can look for pictures or draw pictures of whatever it looks like: a stone wall, a prison fence, a barren desert, the surface of the moon . . . and just accept them as part of our world.

- we can resurrect an image or symbol that once spoke to us and see if it has anything new to say, or whether or not it reopens an

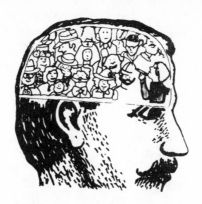

125

old path inward. Some people save special pictures, or have them in past journals; some buy special greeting cards for this purpose, or use the ancient Tarot cards (not for fortune-telling, but for the power of their imagery). The picture just has to be put up somewhere we'll see it.

• draw on all the prayer-triggers or going-within aids we have ever found helpful: music (especially), nature, ritual (homemade or institutionalized), opening to a blank page in our journals and just responding to it whenever it calls (an open blank book staring at us is what is called "invitatory").

• use the body: exercise more regularly, to get the physical dialogue between inner and outer going; the body is a metaphor for the soul.

The reader will note that these aids to opening up the unconscious use, largely, the language of the unconscious: the non-verbal speech of body and image and sound. With these, we say to the less-known part of ourself, "See?—I want to communicate. I'm willing to use your language. Please respond."

Another point to be made about dry times is this—and it is small, but essential. We may be receiving the gift of time for digestion. In approaching the inner world as well as the outer many of us tend to gobble experiences (think of how many vacations for people are hectic times of "seeing all there is to see" or "visiting everyone there is to visit"). The unconscious/God may have sent us a great deal of material, only to have us half-process it, or almost dishonor it in our haste to be on to the next thing. The time when the inner world is remote and silent may be the time we need to go back over our journals and summarize a certain period in our life, or really work with a life-changing dream we only half-appreciated. The inner wisdom knows how much we need these times—or perhaps need time less focused on the inner world to catch up on home and family—and will provide it for us when we neglect to do so.

The opposite of desert-time, when we feel cut off from that home within, are the times we feel inundated by the contents of the unconscious—as though a tidal wave had swept over us. "I'm swamped . . ."—it's as though the channel had been widened to a river's width, and just too much is coming up. We feel as though we're paddling upstream, as dreams and significant daily happenings pour over us. At such times of plenty, we can write

down all the things we need to pay attention to, adding to the list as more items appear. This respects them. Then, we will choose the one that seems most important at the moment—perhaps a recurring fantasy that keeps popping up—and use that as the basis for our active imagination, until its meaning is clear. We can know which is the most important thing with which to deal, because it will carry the largest amount of emotion or affect . . . not necessarily because it has super-important subject matter.

In these swamp-times we really need to pray for a peaceful spirit, knowing that if God is in charge of the process of our homecoming, all will balance out in the end. The other things that seem important to attend to (both inner and outer) will be there— on our list, in our lives—and we will be sent the time to pay attention to them. Remember, we're not the one directing things; our task is to cooperate with grace. Times such as these are valuable lessons for the ego as to Who's in charge and where the center of the personality *really* is—the egocentric person thinks "I can handle it all myself"; the God-centered person knows the true focus of his or her being is not the ego, but its Creator. A home-truth, in more ways than one. . .

Living with Images

We might take a look around our house or apartment. Undoubtedly, there are objects and pictures and symbols—many of them specifically religious—that we hung on a wall or placed on a table or shelf because something in them appealed to us . . . *once upon a time.* When we first put up that picture of *The Gleaners* or the Fra Angelico angel cousin Susie brought back from Florence, we admired it several times a day. Now, it has faded into the wallpaper, barely noticed in our daily rounds.

The point is that images—powerful connections to the depths of our soul—lose their power if we don't use them, or when their work in us is done. Jung's psychology has been called "imaginal psychology" as well as the more familiar "analytical psychology," because it truly is centered around the power of the image. (His revisionist, James Hillman, has developed this line of Jung's thought in his "archetypal psychology.")[10] All through *Coming Home* the reader will have found pointers to the centrality of imagery, but the important question here is, "What can we do to keep the key images before us?" Here are some helpful suggestions:

- keep a box somewhere into which you put evocative pictures wherever they are found (they might come from magazines, from greeting cards, on postcards, from art reproductions at the local museum and many other sources, and can be large or small, colored or black and white; a good source is inexpensive books from tag sales or swap meets which have interesting illustrations). If you have such a collection, when a dream image surfaces you may find something close to it in the box, or something related— a "next step" in your exploration of the particular symbolic image.

- when an important symbol speaks out to you (from within or without), find a picture of it or draw one and put it where you can see it. Live with it, dialogue with it (as suggested above in the active imagination ideas), and perhaps let it find its way to your journal when you have made it your own.

- even if you're not a skillful photographer, anyone can use one of the world's most marvelous inventions, the Polaroid camera. Keep yours with you, prepared to snap a shot of something that stirs up affect in your soul; watch the picture develop in front of you and then use it in any of the many ways suggested here.

- train yourself to see symbolic images in the world through which you move daily: is there a gas station at the corner with a big red star? or a flying horse? does the corner florist also have a picture of the god Hermes (Mercury) in the window? does the railway car passing through the junction have on it the yin-yang symbol or a mandala in the shape of a target? on the supermarket shelves you pass regularly, are there not pictures of animals on tea boxes, mermaids on tuna fish cans, candles, circular breads, magazine covers with titles that can have deeper meanings, and on and on and on . . .? (Yes, this *could* turn a quick run to the store into a two-hour image hunt.)

- in Chapter Seven, there are many examples of that basic pattern, the mandala, to be found in nature and the world around us. Can you rotate pictures of these and others, using them as centering devices, reminders of the kingdom within?

Not just any images will do. We're looking for those which represent something residing in the soul, a deeper part of ourselves. Once we begin to look for them and look at them and live with them, we have a marvelous way of dialogue with the unconscious layers of the soul, which is the natural home of the visual.

The Spiritual Journal

There's been a lot written about journal-keeping, some of it making the practice seem very burdensome. New journalers ask if they need write in their blank books daily; the answer is no. Others ask if a dream log and the journal are the same thing; the answer is that they can be, but perhaps the purposes of logging dreams and keeping a journal are better met if kept separate. Another frequent question is "does the sort of blank book I use for a journal make a difference?"; one experienced recorder tells her story:

"When I was in my twenties, I used to write in spiral notebooks about what was going on in my life. These were really diaries of outer events more than inner journals, but I also recorded my feelings about things and wove some prayers of my own into the pages.

One Christmas, my brother John gave me a beautiful blank book for a present. It had a deep yellow cloth cover with gold stamped borders, and fancy end papers that looked like marble or watered silk. And the paper was heavy, like art paper, so that you could use paints or marking pens on it and they wouldn't show through. It was very special, and larger than the little school-type notebooks I had been using all along. . . but the trouble was that it was too special! I didn't think I had anything to write that was good enough to put in such a beautiful blank book. And so, it just sat there on my desk for—I guess—over a year.

Then one day, when I least expected something wonderful to happen, I fell in love! And my whole world was changed—trees began to sing, and everyone looked beautiful. . . all the clichés about being in love became true. All the songs on the radio were written, I knew, just for me.

It was then that I wanted a special place to put down what was happening to me, and the gold journal was just the right place. My feelings deserved a beautiful container like that, and I filled it with our story, and pictures from magazines, and lyrics of songs, and my fervent prayers that what we had going would last.

Well, to make a long story short, our relationship didn't last (which was a good thing, as he decided later on to be a bookie)—but it certainly got me started on using a large blank book for my journal. After I had seen how rich the everyday events of my life could be, I knew that whatever I might record had value—and needed a vessel that would truly honor it.

I watch for beautiful journals like my gold one (stores usually carry them before Christmas), or I get bound blank books in art stores and paste a picture on the cover, or sometimes when I feel more organized (or when there's a lot to record) I get a nice binder that will hold typewritten pages and blank paper too. I keep colored pencils and some old magazines and glue and scissors nearby my desk, and use them just for journal-keeping. I guess I only put something in my book a couple of times a week now, but it's a special friend and very much a part of my life.

What I've learned is that my insides respond to the way I treat them—that's not a very good way to put it, but I think you know what I mean."

The journal is the place for the active imagination dialogues and the sketches or collages one might make to amplify an inner or outer image. Our dream logs usually get pretty messy, for we write in them when half-awake; they can be the inexpensive notebooks . . . but in the journal go the special dreams, the ones we want to hold close to us so we can feel their heartbeats and make them ours. They can be illustrated there in the journal, and the associations and learnings we have come up with for them will be there too.

Once people have kept a journal or inner diary, they see clearly where they've been on reading it over—and how much closer they are to the goal of knowing their inner homes. On a day-to-day basis, we may think we're getting nowhere spiritually, or even going backwards. . . and then an afternoon spent with the journal of three or four years ago will tell a different story. We may not have become as conscious as we had once hoped we would, but we also know we're not where we were when we began the inner journey.

There are fine books on spiritual journal-keeping, just as there are on dreams as a way of knowing our souls[11]—but the very best thing one can do is begin to keep a journal and allow it to become the mirror of one's odyssey. There are a few suggestions for keeping a journal in "Journal-Keeping: A Special Aid to Spiritual Growth" at the end of this chapter. We need a place for the inner contents to be collected if they are to stay with us and not slip back into the sea.

The Spiritual Friend

The inward journey can be lonely, especially if one has chosen to go through the narrow gate which only admits individuals seeking their particular path. It can also be risky; the deep waters of the unconscious can rise up and overwhelm us, and the creatures who dwell in the depths are not all gentle fishes—sharks live there too.

It was for these reasons that C. G. Jung spoke of the necessity of not traveling alone. He saw the trained guide as an essential part of the analytical process—and, indeed, those of us who can find such a person (whether it be Jungian analyst or spiritual director) are certainly fortunate. However, there may not be that other person; or, if there is, he or she may be beyond our means financially. In today's churches the people who are effective spiritual directors are often way overbooked, with long waiting lists. Does this mean we cannot or should not venture out on our own?

No, it doesn't mean that at all. We must remember that we are speaking of journeying to the home within in a religious context, and we venture forth on that journey with faith in the Spirit, God's indwelling presence. We also have the sacraments of our church (if we are part of a sacramental church) and the rituals of our faith to sustain us.

Two suggestions for those who do not have the trained guide who will walk with them on the homeward road:

1. don't give up praying for and searching for the right person, even if it means revising your ideas of just what sort of person that might be and how far you might have to go to work with him or her (a drive of an hour or more each way, once a month, isn't

unusual—and gives a nice distance from one's everyday world that brackets the set-apart time with the spiritual teacher, saying "this is special"; it also gives one time to think about and process the shared inner contents).

2. be sure to find *someone* with whom you can share your inner explorations, a prayer partner or another seeker or guide with whom you will *make a commitment to meet regularly for this purpose*— and at those times you might:

- catch up on outer news that has any bearing on your soul-lives

- share journal highlights since you last met

- pray for each other's needs

- do exercises from any of the many books that have inner explorations sections (perhaps the journal pages from this book would be a good take-off point)

- read scripture, reflect on it, break the word

- even celebrate, with home-made rituals, special times in the life of either of you: ups, downs, turning points (we all have the trappings of ritual at hand: candles, flowers, gifts, food and drink, pictures, music, incense, God's word). Such celebrations can be geared to a theme that's important to one or both of you, and can include ritual actions such as burying or burning (the past), throwing away (that which needs to be let go of), ingesting (something that needs to be assimilated), and so on; we are limited by our creativity in designing such special times.

Like the journal, time spent with either a spiritual guide or the prayer partner (or, for the fortunate, both) helps us be more objective about our own inner life. It's as though both journal and friend hold up a mirror so we can see ourselves from a distance and

say, "Oh, so that's how I look . . ."; we are too close to our own lives to see them in this detached way. And this objectivity helps us sense more clearly what it is that God is calling us to at this point in our life story.

The special other person—which might well be spouse or older child—helps us in another way. When we share our soul, we develop intimacy with another person—and intimacy, an often misused word, means "to behold another at his or her depths." Being known at our depths is an experience that brings freedom, and healing, peace, nourishment, love, and the letting go of facades—these are the qualities of scriptural home and inner home we investigated in Chapter Three, aren't they? The intimacy between two people in a spiritual friend relationship (whether it be focused on just one of them, or whether time is equally shared) grows as they listen, pray, affirm and support each other, laugh and cry and rejoice together. This is a very special, bonded relationship; with its sense of containment, it becomes like the alchemical vessel that holds together all the ingredients for transformation.

The good books in print on the spiritual friend (or "soul-friend," a gracious term) can help us clarify for ourselves just what sort of special other person would be best for us at this time.[12] They all make the point that spiritual guidance is not to be confused with pastoral counseling or therapy, and that is important. The therapist too can be this sort of companion on the inner way (to use Morton Kelsey's term), but the focus in a counseling situation is on removing roadblocks and finishing unfinished business that acts as a ball and chain to the pilgrim.

"When two or three are gathered together. . . .", said Jesus, good things happen. We need not and should not try to travel home all by ourselves.

Finding Ourselves in Favorite Stories

   Many readers will be familiar with relational Bible study, as popularized in our day by Lyman Coleman in his popular *Serendipity* format (his roots being well-sunk into Ignatian tradition). We have walked with Peter on the water, stood at the foot of the cross, trekked with Moses and the people of Israel through the desert. The Bible stories will always be powerful carriers of many levels of meaning for us—but, sometimes, they have the disadvantage of being *so* familiar that we need to give them a rest. They still teach, but have become very much part of our consciousness . . . thereby failing to be links to the unconscious for us.

   Another valuable source of stories is the folklore of the world, particularly those fairy tales and myths and legends which have been handed down by oral tradition (some of which may be specifically religious in nature, many of which are not). Just as we found with pictures, certain stories draw us to them; that tells us that they have become hooks for our projections in some way.

   Remember, the psyche is constantly tending toward wholeness and balance, and is, therefore, sending us clues about "that which is missing." This is called the compensatory functioning of the psyche, and we see it operating in dreams every night. Bringing those missing parts of ourselves to consciousness, or "redeeming them" from below the water line, is our way of cooperating with God in creation. A story—of any kind—that grabs us is giving us a clue about what's missing from our conscious attitude. Those which we call folklore are especially valuable, because they spring from a primitive, simpler level than the refined and more conscious creation of one person's mind (e.g., the novel, most t.v. series, etc.).

People have always told their stories. The continuous repetition of a favorite tribal myth or national legend ensured its sinking down into the hearts of a people (which American, for example, does not have a mental picture of George Washington cutting down the cherry tree or Abraham Lincoln reading by fire light?). In addition to hearing and responding emotionally to favorite tales, we can see them as descriptions of processes of change within us, and understand that we are attracted to this or that story because it mirrors something going on (or needing to go on) within us at this time. Looking at the story (any story) this way, we see it as a reflector of the transformation process taking place within us. . . . something is always in need of being born.

A story, then, is a more complete projective "hook" than a picture or a person. It is full of images, and it has a beginning, an unfolding, and an ending which describe an entire process within us. When we want to hear or see a story over and over (or when one of our children wants to be read *Goldilocks and the Three Bears* for the fortieth time), it's because we still haven't finished the process of change described in that story. Conversely, when a story we once loved becomes boring or fails to attract us, it's because the situation it pictures is no longer applicable to our soul-life. The "favorite story" changes as we change.

At the end of this chapter there are details on all this in "5 Steps for Unlocking a Favorite Story." We might spend a year or five years on one story, or even have a life myth with many sub-stories. These pages are followed by "Fairy Tales . . . A Bibliography," which includes some references to mythology and legendry, as well as composed and fairy-tale-like stories. Although the skills described can be used with any story, the simplicity of the fairy tale and its nearness to us in time makes it a perfect aid for learning the skills, which can then be applied to a biblical tale (in a somewhat different way from the relational Bible study we are used to), soap opera, or the latest science fiction novel that might attract us. The Greeks say, "the fairy tale has no landlord," meaning it is as much ours as anyone's—but the important point about finding ourselves in stories is to begin with the one that is calling us *now*.

Becoming the spiritual detective is an acquired skill. When we first begin the explorations of the psyche, we may feel in a strange place—just as any new home feels strange at first. Then, with time, we learn our way around, just as we are soon able to find our way around a new home in the dark. And the spiritual seeker learns how to let the inner and the outer worlds in which he or she moves become two parts of one whole, so that they are continually informing each other. This is how we find our way to the center of the home within us, the place where God lives and waits for us.[13]

"I thought I was doing pretty well with my inner life, especially in the years since our children left home and we had more time to ourselves. Then, four years ago my Lily died and I had a mild stroke. The kids decided I shouldn't live alone in the big old house where they had grown up, and I didn't want to live with any of them—so I ended up in this little apartment.

Up until the day they moved me, I felt as though I really had my finger on the pulse of my spirit—even when I was sick, and especially when my wife passed on, I could always pray, and most of the time I wrote in my little book here. My grandfather had taught me, long ago, about pain and suffering. He used to say 'those who are thrown in the furnace come out either burned to bitterness or refined into gold.' Hard times never kept me from God, but once I left our house and was in this strange new place, I just felt as though I was cut off from my soul. It was really terrible. It was as though only half of me was here as I unpacked the boxes and put up pictures.

It took me about six months to get back into feeling I was with the Lord, that I even had an inner life. I guess when they pulled up my physical roots the spiritual ones came with them—and I've had to grow new ones. Now I'm back to being able to stay in touch with God off and on all day, and at night too—you know, when you get older you don't always sleep so well. It's good prayer time."

To everything there is a season.

SPRING, SUMMER, AUTUMN,

Personal Journal Pages
Charting the Path

The story of *The Twelve Dancing Princesses* in this chapter gave a picture of going into a dark place. Let me explore that motif in my own life:

Does this story seem in any way to be mine?

WINTER.

Are there any other stories—fairy tales or other childhood stories, or t.v. or radio shows, or movies, or family yarns—to which I can recall myself being drawn that have this same going-into-the-dark-place theme?

Perhaps I have lived out this motif in my life in some way. What dark places have I ever gone into . . . outer places? (dark basement or attic? closet, garage, hillside cave?) inner places? What were my feelings about these places?

Do any of the dark-places-explorers mentioned at the opening of this chapter (treasure hunter, detective, archaeologist, miner, cave-explorer) fit me? As I approach the mystery that is my soul, what kind of image best describes me?

Can I find a picture or draw a picture of myself as this sort of searcher-in-the-dark? If so, spending some time with it so it can do its churning up within will be time well spent.

There are many, many skills of spiritual growth, only a few of which have been discussed in this chapter. Here is a checklist to help me see the possibilities, choose those most valuable to me now—and collect some ideas for the future. I can star those that are my best aids.

	I have done/had this before, regularly	I am doing/have this now, regularly	This is something I want to do or have in the future
PRAYER:			
liturgical worship	———	———	———
formal (from a book)	———	———	———
quiet and still	———	———	———
shared, group	———	———	———
repetitive (like rosary)	———	———	———
scripture	———	———	———
sung	———	———	———
written	———	———	———
meditative	———	———	———
awareness of God's presence through the day	———	———	———
SACRAMENTAL LIFE:			
living sacramentally (that is, seeing the sacred all around)	———	———	———
awareness of myself as sacrament	———	———	———
relationship to Jesus as the sacrament of God	———	———	———
Eucharist	———	———	———
Reconciliation	———	———	———
Baptism renewal	———	———	———
Confirmation renewal	———	———	———
Marriage, Holy Orders renewal	———	———	———
Healing of sick (when appropriate)	———	———	———

	I have done/had this before, regularly	I am doing/have this now, regularly	This is something I want to do or have in the future
SPIRITUAL READING:			
scripture	_____	_____	_____
other	_____	_____	_____
exploring my favorite stories	_____	_____	_____
LOVING:			
God	_____	_____	_____
myself	_____	_____	_____
others	_____	_____	_____
SPACE APART:[14]			
space for prayer, sanctuary	_____	_____	_____
energy spots, power points —for recharging	_____	_____	_____
SUPPORT PEOPLE:			
prayer partner	_____	_____	_____
spiritual guide	_____	_____	_____
sharing community/ group	_____	_____	_____
vibrant parish	_____	_____	_____
models, heroes	_____	_____	_____
THE ARTS:			
my own creating	_____	_____	_____
appreciating others' work	_____	_____	_____
MEDITATION:			
active (while doing daily activities)	_____	_____	_____
passive (time out)	_____	_____	_____
DREAMS:			
recalling	_____	_____	_____
appreciating	_____	_____	_____
working with	_____	_____	_____

	I have done/had this before, regularly	I am doing/have this now, regularly	This is something I want to do or have in the future
ACTIVE IMAGINATION WITH PERSONAL IMAGES:			
dialogue	————	————	————
drawing/painting	————	————	————
movement, acting out	————	————	————
sculpting	————	————	————
woodworking	————	————	————
poetry	————	————	————
collage	————	————	————
making music	————	————	————
fantasy, story-making	————	————	————
JOURNAL-KEEPING	————	————	————
CARE OF THE BODY:			
enough sleep, relaxation	————	————	————
enough exercise	————	————	————
good foods	————	————	————
self-appreciation	————	————	————
integrated sexuality	————	————	————
stress-reduction (in whatever ways are possible)	————	————	————
regular check-ups	————	————	————
EDUCATION, CONTINUING	————	————	————
SPIRIT OF POVERTY:			
assessment of buying habits	————	————	————
assessment of possessions, needs, attachments	————	————	————

	I have done/had this before, regularly	I am doing/have this now, regularly	This is something I want to do or have in the future
acceptance of lack, embracing the cross when necessary	_____	_____	_____
sharing with the needy	_____	_____	_____

MINISTRY/"RIGHT LIVELIHOOD":

assessment of how my gifts are being used	_____	_____	_____
assessment of fruits of my work/service	_____	_____	_____
burnout prevention	_____	_____	_____
sources of feedback and evaluation	_____	_____	_____
developing the ability to say "no"	_____	_____	_____

SANCTIFYING MY TIME:

offering each day	_____	_____	_____
following the liturgical year	_____	_____	_____
following the calendar year	_____	_____	_____
daily and weekly "oasis time"	_____	_____	_____
away-time, retreat	_____	_____	_____
vacation time when all this goes on hold	_____	_____	_____

Could I purchase a special blank book in which to record and illustrate the most precious soul-gifts I have been sent in my lifetime? In it might go the life-directing dreams that carry their special numinous quality, and personal encounters that were to direct or re-direct the course of my life, and songs that have been my special songs—poems, books, other music too. Fictional characters who have hooked me deserve a page each, as do public figures to whom I have unaccountably been drawn.

This is one way I might honor my inner world and keep a record of its epiphanies. It will be of most help, perhaps, when I feel cut off from that inner world and need to get back to it.

Here is the story of a woman who designed her own mini-ritual to celebrate an inner passage of her life. Does it give me any ideas as to how I might do something similar for some important time or theme in my own inner life?

"We had had a cold and wet winter, the kind of weather that goes to the bone, you'd say. Everyone had had a round of the flu and, just when they thought they'd finished with it, it seemed to come back for another siege.

It had been a time for me of feeling pulled apart—I just couldn't seem to get a handle on all the parts of my life. You know how that fragmented feeling is, don't you?

However, about the end of January, a real change took place in me. I felt as though the pieces came together, first in my outer life and then in my inner. We had been remodeling the kitchen, and that got finished, thank God! I was able to clean up our home and stop worrying about faucet styles and cabinet finishes and building inspectors.

Then, my dreams (which I had been out of touch with) began to speak to me again, and I felt a real revival of my soul. How good that felt—it was as though I had been cut off from myself and now was joined up again, or like a battery that had gotten run down and now was recharged. I began to draw pictures in my journal, something I hadn't done for a long time.

The 'spiritual friend' who walks with me was happy to hear this news! I realized that she had been concerned over my winter doldrums, and she suggested that we design a small ritual to celebrate the feelings of coming together that I was now experiencing. This is what we did. (She has a special little cabinet with all kinds of things to use in rituals.)

She asked me to pick the theme of the celebration, and I finally decided on 'Things Scattered Are Coming Back Together.' I was to bring to our next session whatever I could find in my own world that would express that theme. At first, I couldn't find anything!—and then I took a look around the house and saw my Dad's old picture of The Gleaners, the peasant folk gathering in the harvest. My sun sign is Virgo, and I have also had for a long time a picture of Mary as the virgin holding a sheaf of wheat, as though she had just been out in the fields collecting grain.

I searched the pages of the bible, and ended up in Jeremiah with all his references to the scattered people of Israel, whom God would re-collect—the people of the diaspora:

'Israel is a scattered flock. . . I will bring them from the north country, and will gather them from the ends of the earth. . .'
(Jer. 50:17, 31:8)

So, I had two pictures and some scripture, and then two days before our time for the ritual, I had a beautiful dream about a kaleidoscope—you know, the things with the colored glass that kids play with. It was on the ground, all broken, but when I picked it up and looked through the little hole in the end of the tube, all the parts were back in place and the beautiful circle design was perfectly symmetrical. The day I was to go to my friend's house, I stopped by a toy store and bought a little kaleidoscope, and took it with me.

When I arrived, I found she had set up a small altar-like table with a cloth and a candle and bible. The cloth had a busy center, but a large plain border—as though all the things in the center had been collected together and held in place by the border.

On the table also was a green vase with some dried seed pods in it. You could tell that if you touched them, all the little seeds inside would tumble out. They were the perfect decoration for our theme.

The way we celebrated our ritual was—well, we just did it. We sat one on each side of the table, joined hands and prayed—for me it was mostly a prayer of thanksgiving for the scattered time having passed. We had put one of my pictures at each end of the table so we looked at them and talked about them a little, and then she played a song which was new to me but just right for the celebration, Bind Us Together, Lord.

Then, we read the scripture passages I had chosen and we took turns looking through the kaleidoscope and sharing the pictures it made. Finally, my friend brought out a little mini-feast she had prepared—to go with the theme of collecting things together, she had slices of fruit cake and glasses of mixed fruit punch! We ate it ceremoniously, then ended our celebration by praying again, praying this time that the new phase of coming together in my life would bear fruit for myself and for others. She blessed me and that was our celebration. It was beautiful. This happened many years ago, but I've never forgotten that day—and when I've had other times of feeling pulled in a hundred different directions, I think back to our ritual, and I know that after fragmenting came re-gluing, or whatever you want to call it. I still use my kaleidoscope to remind me of that.''

SOME ADDED THOUGHTS

6 STEPS FOR HONORING YOUR DREAMS

1. Record the dream: Write down all the details, feelings and fine points of each dream. Dating them is helpful.

2. Write down any associations you have for anything in the dream: What connections or memories do the people or things or places in the dream have for you? (for example: a dream of my grandparents' home might stir up memories of peace and security and love–or it might have completely different associations.)

Perhaps the dream seems to parallel some story you know (for example: a dream about being sent out into unknown territory might remind you of stories as different as those of Abraham or the voyages of the Starship *Enterprise*.)

There are books of symbols that can give you background about how people of all times and places have used various images which may occur in dreams. (e.g. *Dictionary of Symbols* by Cirlot)

3. Do something with the dream—Draw it, or write a dialogue with one of the characters or symbols from the dream, or use a picture (drawn or mental) of something from the dream as a prayer-starter.

This will help unlock the meaning of the dream.

4. Listen to the dream as if it were a play or a movie or scripture story: If I saw this on the stage or in a theatre, what would it be about? Can you state the *theme* of the dream in a sentence?

Viewing a dream objectively in this way often helps it to release its meaning.

5. Try to discern what the message of the dream is: Dreams have a purpose; they inform us about things we aren't conscious of in waking life. (This is called the *compensatory* function of the dream.)

What does the unconscious/what does God want me to become conscious of through this dream? You will know you have it right when there is a feeling of sureness, a "click".

6. Response: What action can I take to respond to the dream message or teaching? If we do something in response to a dream, we will often experience a release of energy; the dream shows us another step in the process of spiritual growth.

Throughout the process, prayer and sharing with one's spiritual guide help greatly.

From: *Coming Home: A Handbook for Exploring the Sanctuary Within*. Copyright © 1986 by Betsy Caprio and Thomas M. Hedberg, S.D.B. Used by permission.

ACTIVE IMAGINATION

O.K. I've met this inner witch (critic, brat, etc.) in my dreams and/or in projected form—now, what do I do with it?

We-l-l-l-l—just what you'd do with an outer person or animal or, even, object (or feeling or mood) you need to be in relationship with. . . . Get to know 'em, listen to 'em, befriend them, care for them.

Here are some of the ways you can do that:

Dialogue (in your journal or on tape, or in your imagination)–get in a calmed state and hold a conversation with the person (or object), allowing the feelings and thoughts of him/her/it to bubble up from within. For example:

B–"Well, you old witch, you certainly don't act very well–why do you shriek and howl like that?"

W–"It's the only way I can get your attention."

B–"Oh. Well–you've got it. What do you want to tell me about yourself?"

W–"I'm mad. . . . "

and so on. The inner voice will have surprising things to say–just put them down *without* editing.

Acting Out. Is there some place you could allow the inner character to be expressed? An enemy soldier (or army) in your dreams could, perhaps, be taken to the tennis court or gym or aerobics class, and given a workout. An inner critic could read a book with you, or watch a t.v. program, or get on top of local or national politics–and be asked his or her opinion.

Chances to dress up and *really* act the part are great!–can you be a Hallowe'en witch? a clown of some kind? Could you dance/move as the inner person(s) might?

Art as a way of getting the inner figure *out there*–so it can be seen and related to. You can draw, paint, sculpt in clay, make sand pictures, collage. At the very least, a picture can be sketched of the image and put where you will see it often. Just live with it, let it speak to you (Jung's "carry it in your pocket"). Or, find a special place/chair/spot for it/him/her to stay.

Important figures/animals/objects from within can have special journal sections–or even an entire book to themselves, in which we

- flesh out a description of them, with pictures (how they act, look; their name)

- work up their biographies: what are the roots of this person/thing in us?

- record the times he/she/it manifests itself/himself/herself. How does it act in me?

  This can be an ongoing record–*and we will note how the inner figure changes*.

- put other incarnations of the same archetypal figure, from stories, Scripture, movies, t.v., etc. (amplification)

- record dialogues with the inner figure, especially about his/her/its feelings and ours–and the limitations we must impose on this part of ourselves (e.g. "O.k., Inner Critic, I know you see everything wrong with how I cleaned the house–but I don't want to hear it.")

- delight in the plusses this character inside has brought to our nature and thank it for this

150

- accept the minuses it/he/she has brought us

- record prayer for and about this part of ourselves

The Goal: *To make the inner figure conscious. . . .* and help it *stay* conscious. If we neglect an important part of ourselves that has surfaced to consciousness once, it often repeats its unconscious behavior and we have to start over again to get to know it/her/him.

From: *Coming Home: A Handbook for Exploring the Sanctuary Within.* Copyright © 1986 by Betsy Caprio and Thomas M. Hedberg, S.D.B. Used by permission.

JOURNAL-KEEPING: A SPECIAL AID TO SPIRITUAL GROWTH

Everyone will develop his or her unique style of journal-keeping . . . so here are just a few suggestions. Please experiment until you find what's best for you.

Suggestion #1: Use something for a journal that does honor and respect to its contents–that is, to your soul and its growth. What we use as a journal says something about how much we value the soul.

Suggestion #2: Be creative. . . . since there are no rules as to what can go in your journal, experiment with many sorts of things, such as:

- records of important events in your life

- favorite quotes or sayings or lines from songs

- Scripture passages that suddenly catch you up

- important dreams (you may find you need a more informal dream log by your bed for recording dreams)

- pictures that illustrate your dreams

- other drawings or pictures you have cut out

- questions

- answers

- memories that resurface and need to be tended to

- personal symbols: images that speak to you and your associations and amplications for them, plus active imagination with them in one of several forms (e.g. dialogue, drawing, etc.)

151

- feelings that surface, and some notes about the triggers to those feelings if you know them. . . . also some "fleshing out" of the feeling (what does it look like? say?)

- summaries and reviews of segments of your life. Time lines are helpful here, as are time lines with projections for the future (always write these in pencil!)

- "coincidences": those synchronistic things that happen "by accident."

- prayers, conversations with God
  and much, much more

Suggestion #3: Read some of the famous journals of history and see how helpful the process of journal-keeping was to the writer as he or she developed. Some of these are:
Confessions–Augustine
Journal of a Soul–Pope John XXIII
Markings–Dag Hammarskjöld
Memories, Dreams, Reflections–C.G. Jung
Gift From the Sea–Anne Morrow Lindbergh
Autobiography–Teresa of Avila
Autobiography–Thérèse of Lisieux
The Seven Storey Mountain–Thomas Merton
Diary–Anne Frank
and many more.

From: *Coming Home: A Handbook for Exploring the Sanctuary Within.* Copyright © 1986 by Betsy Caprio and Thomas M. Hedberg, S.D.B. Used by permission.

STORIES: PICTURES OF THE SOUL

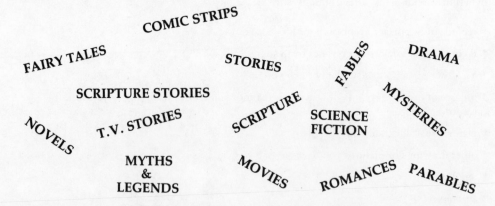

A story can be understood in the same way as a dream–that is, as a carrier of knowledge about the soul. However, it has a beginning, an unfolding of plot, and an ending. A story we are drawn to speaks of *change* within the soul.

The reason a story is a favorite is because it corresponds to something that's going on—or that needs to go on—within us. The story that grabs us is a hook for our projections of something inside that is asking to be made more conscious. When we learn how to understand the correspondence between inner and outer story, we have a valuable tool for self-knowledge and increased consciousness.

TWO BASIC WAYS TO VIEW A STORY
(cf. 2 ways to explore a dream)

1. *Only as inner–*
   (Intrapersonal)

Everything in the story is something *within* the person it depicts. For example, in the fairy tale *Rapunzel*, the young girl in the tower, the sorceress who locks her up, the prince, her parents, and even the tower and the rampion (or lettuce) her mother longs for are seen as ingredients of one psyche.

The events of the story depict a drama of transformation going on within one personality.

2. *Inner & outer–*
   (Both intrapersonal and interpersonal)

We *identify* with one of the characters in the story (e.g. Captain Ahab, Saint Barbara, St. Peter, Jesus, Red Riding Hood, etc.) The other components of the story may be either within us or without (or both).

This method, the more common, has been used by Ignatius in the Spiritual Exercises, by Lyman Coleman and others in their relational Bible study, by Eric Berne for his T.A. Life Scripts, and by many others.

5 STEPS FOR UNLOCKING A FAVORITE STORY
(an intrapsychic approach, the first of the two ways cited above, based primarily on the style of Dr. Meredith Mitchell of Los Angeles and also the work of Dr. Marie-Louise von Franz.)

Stories that have come to us through oral tradition–RELIGIOUS STORIES, MYTHS and FAIRY TALES–tell especially about transformation within a personality.

Step 1: Record the story *as remembered*. What in the story draws or repels you to/from it?

Step 2: The Title. This tells the most important thing activated in the personality at this time, and/or summarizes the message of the story. Associate and amplify (with research) the images of the title, then try to boil down into psychospiritual language (e.g. *The Golden Bird* = s *a most precious flight of spirit*)

GOLDEN
BIRD

Step 3: Overview of the Story. Look at the story as a whole. Usually, it will be in four parts, about movement from one inner condition [at the beginning] to something more developed [at the end]. (Some stories, however, are about regression, or standing still)

INITIAL CONDITION, SETTING (who, when, what, how?)	EXPOSITION, or DEVELOPMENT OF PLOT, "PERIPETEIA" (longest)	CLIMAX or CULMINATION	ENDING or LYSIS: FINAL CONDITION or OUTCOME
A picture of the soul as it is now: what's missing that needs redemption? or what is the conflict/imbalance that needs to be resolved? what is the problem?	The ups and downs, which aid or impede the transformation process. What triggers the action?	The height of the tension. Something happens or changes, giving insight into what has come before.	Result(s): more conscious, stable? less? no change? How does the change affect the life in this personality?

This can lead to the general statement:
"In the personality illustrated by this story, an initial imbalance of _____ leads to a transformation process (or redemption) resulting in the illustrated final condition, which is _____."

Therefore, someone attracted to this story has something similar going on inside. . . . and the details of how the change or transformation is made *in the story* can help one discover how to do the same in his/her life . . . thereby taking more responsibility for it.

Step 4: Work through the story, keeping a consistent attitude, at 3 levels:

- *The Images*–how does each contribute to the outcome (or impede it)? What are my associations for people, animals, things, events (just as for dreams)?

- *Their Meaning in the Psyche*–What in me feels/acts like that? (each thing in the story stands for something in the psyche and acts in accordance with its own principle or purpose.) Keep in context of how the image acts in *this* story.

- *What That Means in Our Life*–How does this archetype or component of the psyche manifest itself or behave or express its nature? (e.g. "Here is how someone might experience this in their life/behavior. . . . ", "This is what it might be like to take a bite of a poison apple, or _____") No judgments!

Step 5: Using this knowledge (which is the whole point, just as with a dream!):

- In what way is this story–and my understanding of it–about my life?

- Where am I in this story–at the beginning? in the middle? at the ending?

- How can I use what I've learned to bring about the same transformation in my life?

- How can I live out the new, changed life that develops at the end of this tale's process?

- What story is next?–or is this one a "life myth", spanning several sub-stories? (We know we have lived through to the end of a story when it has lost its power to fascinate.)

- How can I keep this story before me, so its gift of consciousness doesn't slip back into unconsciousness? How can I honor it, pay it some homage for what it has taught me?

- How can I thank God for it?

154

FAIRY TALES. . . . A BIBLIOGRAPHY

I. BASIC COLLECTIONS OF FAIRY TALES
(gathered from oral tradition)

- *The Grimm Brothers' Fairy Tales (found in many versions)*
  The nursery tales of Germany, first published in 1812. There are over 200 in the collection, and it is useful to find an edition with the standard numbering (e.g. *Rapunzel* is Grimm #12), as different editions give different names for many of the tales.

- *Hans Christian Andersen's Fairy Tales*
  A curious hybrid of folk tale and created story by the gifted Danish 'dream weaver,' the first of which were published in 1835. Based on the stories of the folk, many of these have been assimilated *into* oral tradition. There are over 150 Andersen tales.

- *The Arabian Nights' Entertainment (or, The Thousand and One Nights)*
  These are the chronicles of the ancient kings of Persia, whose empire extended into Arabia, India, Egypt, Palestine and as far east as China. First translated from Arabic into French in 1704. These are *long* stories.

- *French Fairy Tales*
  The French began collecting and editing their folk tales early on, the two best known collections being those of Countess D'Aulnoy of 1682 and Charles Perrault of 1697. Many are paralleled by the Grimms' tales.

- *The Classic Fairy Tales* by Iona and Peter Opie. (London: Oxford Univ. Press, 1974)
  A superb book giving the first English translation of 24 best-loved tales. Of special importance is the historical background of each story, and an overall survey of how the collecting of these folk tales began. Available in paperback, but the hard-cover version has wonderful colored pictures.

- *The Andrew Lang Fairy Books*–12, available in paperback from Dover Publications, 31 East 2nd St., Mineola, NY 11501 (send for their juvenile book catalog)
  In 1889, *The Blue Fairy Book* by English folklorist Lang appeared. Over the years at the turn of the century it was followed by eleven other "colors" of fairy tales: *Red, Yellow, Green, Grey, Lilac, Olive, Orange, Pink, Brown, Crimson* and *Violet*. They are the most complete collection of fairy tales from all around the world, but without an index.

Plus: collections of the folktales from countries east and west, which are readily available. Notable collections have been made, especially, of Celtic and Irish fairy tales, Norwegian fairy tales (*East of the Sun & West of the Moon*), American Indian fairy tales, Japanese fairy tales, Russian fairy tales.

Related Collections of Stories: (which come under the heading of folklore, but are not considered fairy tales)

- Fables–La Fontaine, Aesop

- Parables–those of Jesus, those of other religious traditions (notably the Muslim Sufis and the Jewish Hasidim)

- Myths–the definition of a myth is that it includes some divine intervention

- Legends–legends are based on historical *fact* (e.g., *The Iliad* and *The Odyssey* sprang from the Trojan War). Legends are usually long and contain many sub-plots (e.g. the Arthurian legends, the Welsh *Mabinogian*, the Finnish *Kalevala*, the Norwegian Peer Gynt tales, the Ring of the Nibelung tales of Germany, Robin Hood tales). All religions also have their own legendry, stories that are "truer-than-true" that have built up around the founders and the saints (e.g. in Christian tradition, the legend of St. Martin of Tours dividing his cloak, of Jesus and Mary and the cherry tree, etc. The medieval *The Golden Legend* by Jacob de Vorignes is a collection of saints' tales).

Also, *composed stories* which are folklore-like, but *not* from oral tradition:

- Romances: composed tales of chivalry from the middle ages and later (e.g. the *Roman de la Rose* of France, 13th century)

- Children's stories of our time: dating back to the 19th century, when the idea began to dawn that childhood was a time to be seen as distinct and precious–not just a diminutive version of adulthood. Many examples: *Alice in Wonderland, Gulliver's Travels, Pinocchio*, George MacDonald and Francis Hodgson Burnett's stories, Frank Baum's OZ series, C.S. Lewis' Narnia stories (several have adult levels too)

- Adult stories of our time: science-fiction, particularly, and also some movies and television series that have become part of our collective mind-set–*Star Trek, E.T., Gone With the Wind* (first in book, then in film version), Sherlock Holmes' stories, many others.

II. WRITINGS ABOUT THE MEANING OF FAIRY TALES:

- Books by Marie-Louise von Franz:
  The Interpretation of Fairy Tales
  Shadow and Evil in Fairy Tales
  The Feminine in Fairy Tales
  Individuation in Fairy Tales
  Redemption Motifs in Fairy Tales
  (Spring Publ., Dallas)
      Dr. von Franz was one of C.G. Jung's closest and most brilliant associates, who began work with him when in her teens and has devoted her life to continuing what he began. Her books are transcriptions of her lectures at the Jung Institute in Küsnacht, Switzerland, and not organized as clearly as one might hope, but filled with rich information. She uses approach #2 on our flyer–seeing fairy tales as both inner and interpersonal.

- *The Uses of Enchantment*, Bruno Bettelheim (New York: Vintage Books, 1977)
      A renowned Freudian, Dr. Bettelheim's gift to us in this book is the valuing of fairy tales for children (and adults). There is a lack of emphasis on the spiritual that those used to Jungian writers have come to expect.

- *Once Upon a Time*, Max Lüthi (Bloomington, Ind.: Indiana University Press, 1976)
      Especially interesting because written by a folklorist, rather than a psychologist.

- *Fairy Tales and Children*, Carl-Heinz Mallet (New York: Schocken Books, 1984)

And this one from an educator, an absolutely delightful interpretation of 4 Grimm's tales (*Hansel and Gretel, Little Red Riding-Hood, The Boy Who Set Out to Learn Fear,* and *The Goose Girl*).

- *Fairy Tales: Allegories of the Inner Life,* Jean C. Cooper (Northamptonshire, G.B. The Aquarian Press, 1983)

   A rich study of the archetypal patterns and symbols in the classic fairy stories.

And what of C.G. Jung himself? Jung touches on fairy tales throughout his collected works, primarily in Volume 9i in the article "The Phenomenology of the Spirit in Fairy Tales" (1948), but this is not an avenue he took off on the way he did with alchemy or the mandala. . . .

   But throughout the writings of his followers one can hardly pick up a book without a fairy tale shedding its light. Two writers who especially have mined this vein in print are Ann Ulanov (with her husband Barry) and Linda Leonard (in *The Wounded Woman*). See also James Hillman's work, and Robert Johnson's approach to the Arthurian legends and mythology.

To Summarize! FAIRY TALES are *one* specie of FOLK STORY, which is just *one* category of *FOLKLORE* which also includes games, customs, art, song, dance, ritual . . . many of which are other ways of telling the fairy tale (e.g. the Child ballads of England, Scotland, and the U.S.)

CHAPTER SIX

Whom Will We Meet on the Way?

The Inhabitants of the Psyche

Our outward journeying through life brings us in contact with all sorts of people, animals, objects, places. The inward journey does the same.

Recall our spiral map of what it is like to be at home inwardly in the earliest days of childhood, then to leave home, and then—for some of us—to turn around and go back to that home within us, God's home. The going-out phase of the journey is a time when we very much need to develop those qualities which will help us to make it in the outer world. If that world is, say, the world of the successful business man, we may leave behind the softer parts of ourself—the side that likes to play, or make music, or just loaf. If, on the other hand, the world to which we are adapting is life as a society matron or young mother involved in the P.T.A., the left-behind qualities would probably be whatever doesn't fit with the current social scene or the world of home and family.

When we turn around and retrace the path we have taken, we begin to meet the parts of ourselves that haven't yet had a chance to come into play. They are our shadow side (which is the same as our biological gender) and our contrasexual side (the energies colored by the opposite gender). How do we meet these hidden parts of our soul?—the primary ways are through our dreams (sleeping and waking) and through projections onto people or things in our waking life. (There are other ways too, but these two are our best sources of information.)

Here are just a few of the possible encounters we may have.

"My Dad was a very gifted man. He's been gone about ten years now, but I have really wonderful memories of him. He was an Episcopal priest, and for many years had a deep interest in Carl Jung's psychology, which he felt could bring a new understanding of our ancient faith.

He taught my brothers and me that there were all sorts of potentialities hidden away in us, and that one of our most important life tasks was to get to know as many of them as we could. I can still hear him saying, 'Boys, it's as though there were a line-up of people and animals and gods and goddesses—and even things—inside each of us. You know the phrase "I stand at the door and knock"—which we usually use about Jesus. Well, these parts of ourself are there, standing at the door between our consciousness and unconsciousness, and they knock. They want to come in, and get to know us, and be accepted, and have a place to express themselves.'

Can you see the picture? We were just teenagers then, and really would rather have been out playing ball or watching t.v. I was impressed by my Dad's seriousness, though, and I knew that he was trying to share with us something of great importance to himself . . . I guess that's what made me listen.

Well, today at 44, I've come to know what he was talking about. One by one, the people who are in the dark of me have knocked at my inner door. Sometimes I've been glad to know them—the kid who didn't have enough time to play in the snow is one I've welcomed (and let play). Other times it's been very hard to spend time with someone like the jackal who came prowling around my door, or the ranting and furious gang leader I met in a dream. I'd rather not admit they are there . . . but I've learned it's better to let them become conscious and to stay in charge of them (or try to) than to have them roaming around in the dark. They pop out anyway—and in much worse ways—when they aren't paid attention to. Another of my Dad's sayings was, I've since learned, a Jungian byline:

'If you don't work with the unconscious, it will work on you.'[1]

What I've learned over the years is that this isn't unlike having Jesus stand at the door and knock. Surely my little kid who wants to make snowmen and the punk tough guy and all the rest are parts of the Christed self that is me. It's quite a collection, I'll tell you."

161

It's an amusing picture, isn't it?—an infinite line-up of inner characters, waiting at the entrance-way to consciousness. Do they wait patiently, we wonder? Or, perhaps, they are jostling each other (and us) for space near the head of the line. We know when it is the next one's turn because, if we have kept our spiritual-detective antennae fine-tuned, we begin to see everywhere signs of the next part of ourselves we are to know.

The siren within us, for example, may come up in a dream, and at the same time we may notice that sort of woman on television shows, finding her strangely attractive . . . for the first time. A siren-like woman may come into our life also, and we may find ourselves buying a more-seductive-than-usual outfit for ourself or the woman in our life. The constellation of clues—the too-many-coincidences-to-be-an-accident syndrome—is what tells us that this particular part of ourselves is close to consciousness (or, has moved to the head of the line, to use the clergyman's image).

When we begin to go within, the first parts of ourself we are likely to meet are those nearest to the ego, the other "men within" (if we are a man) or the other "women within" (if we are female). Jung called this the shadow, emphasizing its great value to us.[2] The part of us which is "other"—that is, the opposite gender qualities in us—were probably discarded earlier in our journey outward, and so are now farther away from us. (There is, however, no infallible schedule for the appearance of these inner figures.) Interestingly, but not surprisingly, we catch glimpses of the God in us all along the way home, as the images of the primary and most powerful archetype—the Self, or the image of God dwelling within us—appear and reappear in tantalizing fashion, as if to call us onward. That is just what is happening; we are being called home.

Does it mean, when images of the Self appear in a dream or around us in our daily life, that "we have arrived"? The answer to that question is "no!"; the images of our totality or wholeness appear not because we have it all together but because *we need to pay attention to* that wholeness. (C. G. Jung spoke of the healing power of the mandala, one of the images of wholeness which often appears spontaneously when we most need our fragmented parts to come together.) The images of the Self appear when we need to bring this total picture to consciousness; knowing where we're going—or, to use our primary metaphor, having a glimpse of the home toward which we are headed—makes all the difference as we journey.

Without the goal in sight (at least, to the eyes of the heart), we travel blindly.

We have already met some of the visual symbols of the Self in our pages:

- the idea of home, and of coming home

- the mandala, especially in its representation by biblical images of places of rest

- the motif of four-ness

- the extraordinary person, like the old woman at the foot of the stairs.

Here is a story of another extraordinary inner figure, who—because she was the product of a woman's psyche—seems to represent the very core of her being.

"Many years ago I had a dream which is as real to me today as the night I dreamt it. I had scheduled a first visit to a spiritual director, a man I had been hoping to work with for some time. It was to be, I hoped, the beginning of a new phase of my spiritual life. The night before our first meeting, I had this dream:

The Sea-Companion

I am in ancient Greece, on the Aegean Sea. I approach a sandstone colored temple-like building, and go up the few steps to the colonnade. From there I can see the incredibly blue-green sea, lapping up at the base of the temple. As I am watching the waves I see, far out, a beautiful woman begin to emerge from the water. She has long brown hair, and a blue-green dress which has branches of seaweed trailing over it. Even though she's soaking wet, her hair is all in place and her dress looks perfect, with no wrinkles the way you might expect if one was dripping her way out of the sea.

She comes through the waters gracefully, right up to where I'm standing and says, 'I am your soul-friend.' 'Oh,' I reply, 'I thought I was here to see Mr. _____.' She just smiles, then pulls out some balloons and bubble gum, of all things! As the dream ends, I realize that we are going to spend time together playing like girls of seven or eight.

Her name is Delight.

Well, you can imagine how deeply such a soul-friend, who came to me while I was sleeping, touched me. She was so real! I knew she was a goddess, and yet she seemed so human, so much fun. The name 'Delight' really suited her. I thought about her all day, and when I finally got to the office of the spiritual director, I was still so wrapped up in my inner sea-companion that I had lost my anxiousness about meeting him.

Although I had planned to start off with something completely different, I found myself rushing into the story of my dream. He asked me to repeat it, listened very carefully—and then this dear man did a most remarkable thing. He pulled up an empty chair to the space where we were both sitting and said, 'This will be Delight's chair. She can help us. She knows all kinds of things I know nothing about.'

Even though she was my inner figure, he was the one who went out of his way to take her most seriously (I still felt a little strange talking about imaginary ladies in empty chairs, but to him she was as real as I was). I told him she reminded me of the pictures of Aphrodite rising from the sea, even though she looked different and was contemporary enough to know about bubble gum! And I sang him a few bars of a song she had brought to mind

'Green was the color she laid upon my hand, like the robes of a queen. . . '

Then, the best thing happened. It was time for me to go. I stood up, shook hands with this new friend for the journey, and he bent over to the empty chair where Delight had been for the past hour and touched the seat—to see if she had left any of the sea water where she had sat! I will never forget that twenty-four hours."

Truly, this sea-goddess is a representation of the Self, a feminine depiction of the God living in the soul of the story-teller. In a man's personality, we would say this dream woman was a representation of the anima, his feminine side. Might she not be the woman-dreamer's shadow, in one of its forms? Possibly, but this dream goddess carries about her a numinosity or holiness—a larger-than-life-ness—which is the trademark of the Self. In addition, the dreamer's reaction of awe and reverence tells us that her beautiful guide from the sea, our original home, is more than a shadow-woman (although they can be very powerful too).[3]

As long as we continue to explore our inner terrain, we will never exhaust the possibilities of encounters with inner figures. . . for the unconscious is as deep as the sea from which the green-clad sea-goddess arose in the dream. We have within us a myriad of inhabitants—and each is a part of us.

Room at the Inn for All

Meeting the inner children or rejected tramps or creatures from other realms is one thing—knowing what to do with them, once encountered, is another!

Our goal with these inner people (or animals or objects) is the same as if they were *outer* people (or animals or objects) with which we wanted to be in relationship: we need to get to know them, to listen to them, befriend them, care for them, ask them questions ("where have you been all my life?"), share our feelings with them. The rules of relationship are pretty much the same whether the one related to is "out there" or "in here." "Reach out and touch someone"—good advice!

Here is where the active imagination techniques we shared in Chapter Five are so helpful. The parts of ourselves that are unconscious will often seem to work against us; they have been left in the dark (Jung says that the psyche has "historical layers which are not just dead dust, but alive and continuously active in everyone")[4]... but when brought into the light and retained there, they share their helpful qualities with us—and we can harness their less desirable aspects and be in charge of them. It's as if we put our arm around, say, the thug who lives inside us and said to him, "Now, I really need your power and energy for I've been feeling very drained and weak—but you can't go around with a chip on your shoulder, always expecting people to be the enemy. Let's see how we can manage as a pair." There is a famous *Star Trek* episode that illustrates this beautifully, in which Captain Kirk gets his logical, humane side separated from his raw, predatory nature. Upon seeing what he thinks is the negative aspect of himself, he rejects it, only to discover that without its energy and strength he is half a man. The episode is titled "The Enemy Within," for this more primitive man seems to be the enemy until Kirk gets to know him. The story ends with the Captain embracing his shadow, saying "I need you."[5]

Jesus spoke of the "enemies within our own household," and this is just what the parts of ourselves to which we are unrelated can become if they are not conscious. The inner figures need to be accepted and loved. They are like refugees, homeless people who got stranded as we journeyed forth. The old Simon and Garfunkel song *Cloudy* has the line, "I left my shadow waiting down the road for me awhile . . . ", and that is just what has happened to the unknown parts of ourselves. . . but they need a home too. They are the ones Jesus told us were hungry and thirsty and naked and in prison, the ones who need caring for.[6]

Sometimes people think these less-than-attractive parts of themselves must be done away with, for our religious traditions have not, for the most part, encouraged us to acknowledge the killer or the tyrant within (much less embrace her or him). Repression, however, doesn't work; facets of ourselves which are not acknowledged pop out anyway, in uncontrolled or unharnessed fashion.

Here is a flow chart one woman made of a Japanese samurai warrior who lived within her psyche; her name for him was "Shogun."

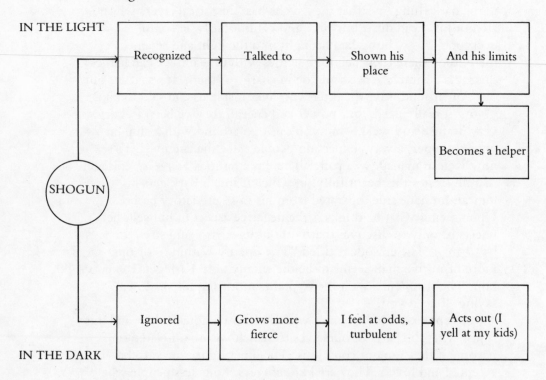

To review, then, when an inner figure becomes very prominent and we can see that it is a major soul-character, we can set aside a section of a journal for it (or even give it an entire book of its own, just as new babies have their special logs), in which we

• describe it thoroughly, with pictures and words showing how it looks and acts

• name it, giving this act of naming the same importance it has in our biblical tradition

• work up its "biography"—that is, trace its development back as far as we can, trying to understand the causes that led to this character's being left in the dark in the first place. For example, in the biography of a foot-stamping inner brat, we could probably all tell of parental rules and regulations which (justifiably) told her or him to keep still. That nasty little kid, however, has a lot of spunk and self-assertiveness, which may be just what we need at age twenty or thirty or sixty.

- keep a running log of the times at which this inner figure emerges ("Today when I had to appear in traffic court, I felt my Pitiful Child come out. . . "). As we keep an ongoing record, we will see the inner figure change; its appearances will be more helpful to us and less detrimental. Soon we will be delighting in the plusses this character adds to our nature, and will be thanking it for helping us. ("This time when I appeared in traffic court, I took my Samurai warrior with me, carefully harnessed, of course, so he wouldn't attack the judge. I really felt strong and wasn't intimidated by having to be there; together we took it in stride. After all, he's known far more terrible experiences than being lectured by someone sitting on a bench. . . but I did have to hold him down a little when the judge said, "One more time and you lose your license.") This kind of record of the inner person's appearances will become for us a barometer of our developing (or receding) consciousness of that aspect of ourself. If the quality we're working with is one we have met primarily in the form of projection on someone else our changing relationship to that person becomes the barometer or gauge as we withdraw the projection and reclaim that energy for ourself.

- continue to dialogue with this figure, so that he or she won't slip back under the water line (which is what happens to once-known inner characters we neglect; we have a space in us between consciousness and the unconscious that is like the space on the beach between the tide-lines, and it is the home of many half-known aspects of ourself).

- assess the minuses of this inner character and accept them. We will find ourselves recording such things as "The red knight in me wants to go tearing around crusading all the time. He is restless and disturbing to my spirit. He will need constant reining-in by the quieter parts of myself until such times as I need his energy to come charging out—but that's just the way he is, and that's o.k."

We can record the limits we place on the figure with which we are working. To an Inner Critic, for instance, we might write: "You can come out when I have to look over the term papers I've written, but I don't want you telling me all the things I did wrong every time I meet someone new or go on a date. I don't want to hear it, and that's not your place—*so be quiet.*"

- record prayer that focuses on the person or thing or animal or group to which this special section or book is devoted: "Lord of all creation, you know you made me fearfully, wonderfully, as it says in the psalms. Well, there is this witch. . . and she must be part of your creation too, for she certainly is alive and well right here. But we've got to do something about her. . . "

"*Most of my life has been filled with hatred. I grew up, black, in the deep south of the 1940's—you saw it on Roots, remember? My grandfather had been crippled by a white overseer when he was just a boy, my father and older brother had been lynched by the Klan, and my sister was gang-raped by some good ole' boys in our town—white men, of course. I hated them all.*

It wasn't until I was a grandfather myself that I began to see just how much harm it was doing to me to stay filled with hate. The best part of my life has always been family and church, and I could recall my mother's voice saying, 'Only God can make us love those who treat us so badly.' As a boy and young man, I thought she was crazy to talk like that—but now I see the truth of her words. Hating hurts the hater worst of all. I am asking God now, humbly, to help me stop hating white people and to keep me from letting those old feelings rule the rest of my life."

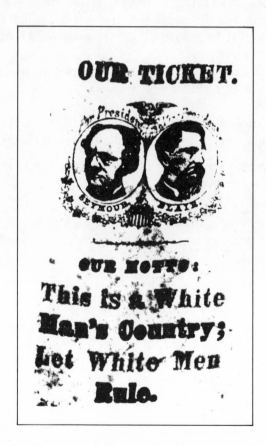

The more unruly inner aspects may need special handling in order to become conscious and stay conscious and even useful. Most of the active imagination we describe here is ego-activity, but it is the Self, that powerful core of our being, that may have to tame or keep in check the really overpowering monsters or demons or hurricanes.

It is God's life in us doing *all* the amalgamating of our many facets, of course, but this needs to be especially explicit in cases of the super-powerful dragons and Nazi generals and Darth Vaders and Medusas within.

There are variables in the way inner figures may appear. Here are some of these, with possible interpretations:

- in *masculine* or *feminine* form, which will relate it to the shadow or animus/anima level of the psyche, depending upon one's gender

- *old* or *young*, indicating energy that has been around awhile, or energy that is new for us

- *friendly* or *unfriendly*, meaning a part of myself that I can be comfortable with, or a part I have rejected (and, therefore, may be antagonistic)

- *mature* or *immature*, the latter indicating something that has to grow up

- *singly* or *in a group*, the former pointing to something that has become more differentiated for us, the latter suggesting that it is associated with the collective and not yet differentiated

- *too little* or *too much*, which would lead us to ask if we were underendowed or being swamped by whatever the quality is

- *very personal* or *very remote*—for example, a family member or friend or ordinary person as contrasted with a person of another race or a god or goddess or someone from a far distant land. The more familiar, the closer to consciousness; the more remote, the deeper into unconsciousness is this figure

• *size variations*, from diminutive or reduced, which might mean it is a quality underdeveloped, or perhaps regressing (for example, a dream of Thumbelina, which might equal little girl qualities not being given enough attention, or perhaps receding after having been tended to)—to oversized or giant-like, which suggests either that this aspect is looming up and needs to be noticed, or that perhaps *too much* space is being given to it

• *primitive* or *very sophisticated and cultivated*, the former pointing to something from a very instinctual level and the latter, to something nearer to consciousness and better integrated into the psyche at this time.

Each of us has a few inner characters that are especially important: for one of us there will be lifelong partnership with a neglected child and a stern schoolmaster; for another, the main sidekicks will be a raging lion and a daredevil trapeze artist. Other people and animals and objects will come along, but the central ones will continue to demand our attention. We want them to *stay* conscious, not have them slip back into darkness and behave unconsciously. When this happens we find ourselves saying things like, "I thought I dealt with you last year." Then the once-attended-to (but now, neglected) inner voice will say, "You did—and then you forgot me." The rules of good relationship we know so well when it comes to family and friends in the outer world are just as true with the inner world. (Fortunately, if we have neglected an inner partner, getting to know him or her again is never as lengthy a process the second—or tenth—time around; it's like renewing an old acquaintance.) We need to keep these relationships alive, and the special journal section or separate journal is a valuable tool for doing so.

The most important inner aspects belong to the God-life within us, the images of the Self that appear. If we attend to them and honor them, we become more and more aware of how we are made in the image and likeness of God, and this centermost part of our being can begin to become the *most* conscious of all the inner beings. Our interior "inn" has room for all. . . and at the center, the Christ-life.

173

. . . And Even the Animals

The words above are from the book of Jonah. The animals of Nineveh, you may recall, were dressed in sackcloth and fasted, just as did the Ninevites when they heard the words of the prophet about repentance. God spared the city, king, people . . . and even the animals, who had shared fully in the penitential activities.

This chapter is about the inhabitants of the psyche, the many inner aspects of ourselves who, unlike the Holy Family at Bethlehem, find room at the inn that is our soul. This phrase reminds us of the Nativity, and the first Christmas scene is one replete with animals—the ass, the oxen surrounding the manger, the sheep. The nativity of our own Christ-life is also surrounded by animals, inner animals, who take part in our development just as the Ninevite animals did with their masters so long ago. Let's linger a moment to take a special look at these unique inhabitants of our own inner world.

We may meet them in dreams, yes—the serpent that unexpectedly appears in our quarters, the bird flying overhead or perched on a tree, the fish or cat or dog or tiger of the night. Even more, in our relationship with the animals of our waking world we meet the animal side of ourself; the mechanism of projection works not just with other people but with the less-than-humans with whom we share the earth.

C. G. Jung says that "animals generally signify the instinctual forces of the unconscious . . . which need to be integrated as part of the individuation process." Further, the great Swiss psychiatrist adds,"…anyone who overlooks the instincts will be ambuscaded by them, and anyone who does not humble himself will be humbled . . . "[7] (which sounds familiar!)

Our name for the person whose animal instincts have ambuscaded him or her is. . . beast. The beast is the animal at its worst, or the person who has turned into an animal. The ultimate beast, repression of the instincts carried to the extreme, is the legendary human who actually turns into a werewolf or a vampire bat or some other creature. Jung is quoted as having said there are

four repressions in our day: sexuality, the creative imagination, nature and animals.[8] Two of these—sexuality and the creative imagination—reside at the level of the instincts deep within us. They cannot be seen—but the world of nature and the animal world in particular *can* be seen, and these become screens upon which we project our relationship to the hidden instinctual side of ourselves.

Some of us have a posture of hatred toward this part of our being. Not aware of this unconscious attitude, we may be the ones who strip-mine countrysides and blithely bulldoze trees and fields, or who misuse animals for experimentation and lock them in cages. Or, if we have a family animal, it may be shut out in the cold, left tied to a chain or confined to a pen and never allowed freedom. This is what we are doing to our inner instinctual nature, so we live out these same repressions outwardly. The outer life reflects the inner.

Many of us are kinder to ourselves and the natural and animal worlds around us, however. In fact, we can be *too* kind, lavishing diamond collars on our cats and showers of baby talk on our poodles. It's as though we knew, without ever thinking about it, that nature and the animals deserve to be cared for—but because we don't know the natural, animal, instinctual side of ourselves and haven't learned how to care for that, we let our pets (or maybe a potted cactus to which we talk at great length, or even a pet rock— plants and minerals being lower octaves of the natural kingdom) carry that tender loving care for us. Again, the instinctual related to only in projected form—but at least cared for, which is a far more enlightened posture than cruel repression.

Think, for a moment, of the animals who have padded or winged or even slithered their ways through your own life, especially those who were such close companions that they were like a part of yourself. Maybe the special loved animal wasn't even alive, but a stuffed toy (which, of course, is very alive, as the velveteen rabbit reminded us). For some, the close animal friends are Snoopy pictures or Garfield notebooks, china horses or cat doorstops of iron, teddy bears on stickers or clothing; these are not

175

one step removed from the living, sentient animal, as is the stuffed toy, but two steps removed. Is it possible that in caring for these real or pictured animals, you have met and cared for instinctual qualities which do indeed reside within yourself, but of which you have not been conscious at the time?[9] (One story tells of the convent of especially gentle nuns whose beloved pet was a vicious, uncontrollable dog capable of striking terror even into the heart of its veterinarian.)

Origen, the famous third century teacher, suggested as much to the people of his day, telling them:

> "Understand that thou hast within thyself flocks of cattle . . .
> flocks of sheep and flocks of goats. . . the birds of the sky are
> also within thee. . . "[10]

The ideal would seem to be loving care for the natural world and the animal kingdom—not repression, not excessive devotion—and, at the same time, tending of the inner configurations to which the animals correspond and of which they remind us: our instinctual nature. Like Adam, we get to name the animals. This is our own "animality" (not such a negative word at all, for the root of it is the Latin *anima*, soul or breath); the instincts do indeed "animate" us. They give us soul.

It is this instinctual side that, recognized, helps us to be at peace with just who we are, in the way, say, the long-legged crane stands motionless and at peace on some marsh. This is how the archetypes within us operate—instinctively; each has its own nature and acts accordingly.

It is our instinctual level that, known, gives us a sense of self-containment and togetherness, in just the way we see that quality mirrored for us by the average house cat, eyes half-shut, who seems to have ageless wisdom residing within her.

176

It is our instinctual nature that accepts sexuality as just one of our many facets, which is the way animals handle sexuality. Those coming from a religious tradition of sexual repression and devaluation may find in the animals far more wholesome models of body-awareness than any human models they have ever been given.[11]

And, to mention just one more of the many possible reasons for our need to stay conscious of our instincts, it is our animal nature that knows what it is to be vulnerable—and to admit it, as a frightened creature of the forest does so wisely. The deer and the wood duck have no need to pretend to be ever-self-sufficient and endlessly strong. They know when to run, when to lie down and rest, when to play.

The numerous saints whose stories are connected to animal life seem to paint a picture for us of good relationship to both inner and outer animality. It is as if their rapport with the creatures testifies to their inner wholeness and acceptance of the instinctual in themselves. We picture Francis and animal life together unfailingly and have legends of dragon-taming (not slaying) saints like Martha and Julia. St. John Bosco with his guardian-dog Grigio is closer to our time, and Jesus, so in touch with all that was natural, used the birds of the air and the ox fallen in the pit to teach those who had ears to hear. In *Compassion*, Matthew Fox has an excellent section on animals in spiritual traditions, citing Jewish Midrash tradition of how "both Moses and David were chosen to lead Israel because of their compassion toward animals." (He follows this section with a fine one on animals as spiritual directors.)[12] Further to the east, similar stories are told of those who are holy: the Buddha is connected to a grey and white cat (based on his awareness that, even asleep, the cat was instinctually tuned in to what was going on) and there is the Hindu holy man who would not enter heaven when he found that his faithful dog was not permitted to follow him. (This latter tale, from the *Mahabharata*, was translated into American mountaineer terms to become a *Twilight Zone* episode.)

"Recently, I learned that I have a serpent inside, of all things! First I had this dream:

I am in a house, familiar but not my own. Ian, my son, is calling for help from the bedroom. He is lying on the floor with a blanket over him and a snake beside him. It looks threatening, poisonous, and I am afraid for him. I think about many ways to kill the snake, like harnessing it with a rope, stabbing it with a knife, etc. I do nothing, and then find myself wrapped around with this very large, heavy, cold green, brown and white snake. This snake is kind and non-threatening, with clear black eyes. Believe it or not, he talked to me and said he was lonely and needed a friend. Would I be his friend and accept his embrace?

Although I'm not afraid, the snake is very heavy—and, also, embarrassing . . . how am I to go anywhere with this snake wrapped around me? I think, 'I'll talk to him, and then when he feels comfortable and sleepy, I'll slide him off and run.' Every time I think this, he tightens his grip on me, as if he can hear me!

I woke from this dream with a stiff neck from looking at the snake. There was no doubt that it was an important dream for me, and I knew I had to do something with it. First I drew some pictures and I also spent time reflecting on how, with the snake wrapped around me, I was less frightened than before—when, you would think, it should have been the opposite. I realized that the snake had 'gotten higher'—or, more conscious. This is what makes the snake-energy less scary. It was obvious from the dream that it wasn't going to let me go.

Well, this wasn't my favorite dream, and I might have forgotten it conveniently—except that the next day I was out running and whom should I pass but a man with his pet snake wrapped around him in just the same way! It was as though a reminder had been sent to me just so I would not ignore my dream.

So, I keep at it. This week I went into a pet store near where I work and spent some time looking at the snake they had for sale there. It looks like my dream serpent, so I'll go in again. I hope they don't sell it before I finish my visits there. Also, I've spent a little time looking at pictures of some of the ancient goddesses, who often had snake friends to show their closeness to the earth."

Animals and home go together, always have. This is true of the first scriptural home we knew, the paradise garden, and of its later allegorical counterpart, the peaceable kingdom. These ancient homes, we have seen, are representations of the inner home within us all—and there too the animals dwell, side by side.

Just as so many of us think of our outer animals as rounding out the family (how many Christmas cards did you get last year that had inscriptions from "Joe and Sally and Jimmy and Fluffy," or something similar?), the inner animals round out the family of soul-inhabitants we've been examining in this chapter. They wait for us along the road to home just as surely as the patient dog or cat waits at the door of our outer home—and they are just as glad to see us when we finally attend to them.

Personal Journal Pages

A Family Portrait

"One year several friends and I shared a program called Centerpoint,[13] which is about how psychology and religion come together. We spent a good deal of time on the various inner figures in each of us, and even concluded the year by having a party for our shadow figures. For that we each chose one of the several 'other people' within us, and came prepared to introduce him or her to the others— through words, or pictures, or even dressed up as the shadow.

You can imagine the collection of people who showed up, can't you? As I recall, there was a witch, a dragon, a little girl, a very sexy street-wise lady of the evening, an absent-minded professor, and a Godfather-type gent in a pin-striped suit with a black shirt and white tie! They all talked to each other, broke bread, and generally had a good time.

When I got home from that party I realized that we had done something very important. We had really made these inner figures clear—brought them into the light, so to speak. . . and they would never again be as vague and shadowy as they had been in the past. The simple act of introducing them to others and sharing how each shadow figure looked and acted will help all of us remember them, always. I felt very sure about that.

Then, the next thought I had was that since this was such a useful thing to do, and since I have quite a few inner figures—most of them people, but some animals too, and some inanimate things—why not do something to keep them before me? My experience has been that I can work hard to help, say, a dream figure become conscious. . . but that he or she slips away and starts acting unconsciously again all too soon. I needed to find some aid to help me pay regular attention to my inner family, just the way I have a list of family birthdays and anniversaries that helps me pay attention to my outer family (believe me, with thirteen grandchildren you really need a system).

Well, on the living room wall I have one of those big picture frames with about twenty spaces in it for small pictures of one's family—you know the kind I mean, don't you? You can get them in any large chain drug store or department store. All our children's pictures are in it, and their children too. You can guess what came next!. . .

I looked at that frame, and I thought 'Why couldn't I do that for my inner family too?'—and I did. I got another frame, this one shaped like a house in fact, and

THE
FAMILY
THAT PLAYS
TOGETHER STAYS
TOGETHER

gradually I've been putting in pictures that I've found in magazines or that I've tried to draw to show the women in me (yes, one is the witch who went to the party), and the men in me, the animals and things too. In the center is the God in me, and the different ways that central energy has come to my attention.

At first, I hid this production in the bedroom closet so no one would see it and wonder if Mom had flipped out. . . but now I've gotten bolder about sharing what works for me, and it's on the bedroom wall. (Anyway, grandmothers are entitled to act a little weird sometimes.) I speak to these folks and try to pay attention to the strengths of each one, saying how I need it in whatever I'm about. Sometimes they have something to say to each other. This way, I feel I stay conscious of them—which is what I want to do.

Years ago I made a cross-stitch sampler for the kitchen that says 'The family that prays together stays together'—I look at it today and know it says something about my inner family as well as my outer!''

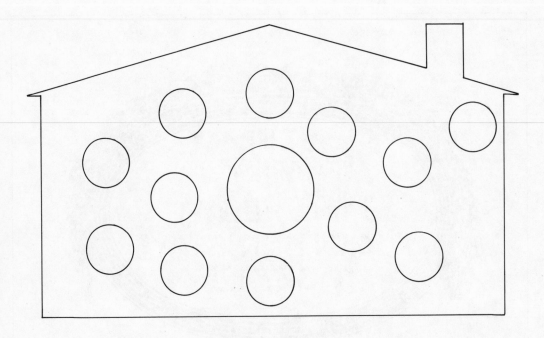

Here is a drawing of a picture frame like the one described by the grandmother, above. Do I have inner figures who could go into the spaces? (It might be helpful to group the inner men and "masculine" animals or objects, and to collect together the inner women and "feminine" animals or objects, as well as giving central space to the God-images that have been uncovered. Jung spoke of how we "circumambulate the self," or come at this core from differing angles.)[14]

If this idea of an inner family portrait appeals to me, could I not get a real picture frame of this style and follow the example of the grandmother who shared her story? (Some have found wall shelves with many little niches serve the same purpose and are even easier to work with. They sometimes come in the shape of houses, which is especially appropriate when using them to display the members of one's inner household.)

Would my motto be the same as hers ("The family that prays together stays together")? Or would it be something else? What are some other possibilities? (e.g. "You can choose your friends but you can't choose your relatives" or "A house divided against itself cannot stand"). Maybe just the title *All in the Family* will do.

182

The animals—both inner and outer—with whom we have shared our lives are important. They can teach us about the more instinctual, less highly developed parts of ourselves. A young girl tells of her friend, her cat:

"One day when I was sitting with Kitty I thought, 'She's not just my friend. She's my teacher too.' So I sat there with her on my lap and made a list of the things I have learned from Kitty. This is my list:

- *She teaches me how to be quiet.*

- *She teaches me how to wait.*

- *She teaches me that it's good to be alone sometimes.*

- *She teaches me that it's good to do things for myself as much as I can.*

- *She teaches me to ask for what I need.*

I showed the list to my older sister, who's fifteen. She said to me, 'You could add that she teaches all of us about feeling good about ourselves—the word is dignity.' And then she said, 'How about showing us the importance of freedom? Cats don't do what they don't want to do.'

I put these on my list and read it to Kitty. She looked up at me with her green eyes as if I wasn't finished. I thought about it and added three more things:

- *She teaches me about gracefulness, like a dancer.*

- *She teaches me about not being self-conscious.*

- *She teaches me that even inside a beautiful creature a killer can lurk (last week she brought home another mole and left it on the doorstep).*

Then she tucked her head under her paw and purred herself to sleep. I am glad I have had a cat for a teacher."

What animals have been important in my life?

- family pets
- other people's animals
- farm animals
- wild animals
- animals in stories or movies or television shows
- dream animals
- make-believe animals

Why have they been important? Have I learned things about myself by meeting them first in animals? Of which have I ever been afraid? With good reason or not? The Book of Job says, "Listen to the animals." Have I done that with any consistency in my life? Looking back over the family portrait of the last exercise, have I included any animals in my collection of inner figures? Could I add some animals to that picture?

—*Homeward Bound*, by
Paul Simon[15]

Part Three

Home, at Last

CHAPTER SEVEN

A Picture of Home

Land of Rest

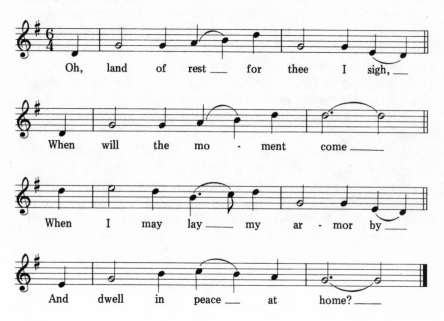

Oh, land of rest ___ for thee I sigh, ___

When will the mo - ment come ___

When I may lay ___ my ar - mor by ___

And dwell in peace ___ at home? ___

Which of us has not had such sentiments? Those who first sang this early American folk hymn[1] knew well the longing for the peace of home. They were referring to the heavenly home, when their toilings in the mountains of Appalachia or across the prairies of the midwest would be done and they could be at rest. We could as easily sing it today, in the concrete canyons of Chicago or New

York or on Main Street, U.S.A., as could peoples all around the globe. Will there ever be a time of rest and peace, a time when we can stop waiting for the next disruption of our lives, a time when we are truly *at home*?

Our book, so far, has described the home within us, the place where God dwells and we have explored at length the journey to that inner home.

It has always been there. It is there now, waiting for our return to it. . . and so, we have to ask this question as we come to the last of our time together in these pages: "Can I be 'at home'—that is, with God—here on this earth, in this lifetime. . . or must I wait (as my ancestors seemed to believe, and sing) until I die?" Being "at home" is just another expression for the ancient goal of the spiritual life: union with God. And the teachings of all the world religions tell us that, yes, we can live that life of intimacy with the divine Lover in this lifetime. It is the state of being which brings us the joy and peace for which we were created—and the rest from turmoil and meaninglessness which we so crave.

In our psychological language, this is described as being Self-centered. (Remember that "Self," with a capital S, is Jung's term for that core of our being that we are calling the dwelling place of God.)

Being "self-centered" (with a small s) means that ego-needs rule the personality. It is the same as egocentricity. Being "Self-centered" means that a well-established ego has allowed itself to become the servant or handmaid of the higher life principle within, and that that Self or God or Universal Truth or Power of Love or the Force (or whatever other words best say it for anyone) is now in charge. We have gotten ourselves (small s selves—or egos) out of the way.

In one sense this sounds so easy, doesn't it? "Of course God is in charge of my life. I have given my life over to God/been born again/renounced my selfish ways. . . etc. etc. etc.," we say. And making that act of faith does, indeed, help us to give ourselves away to our God. Yet, the act of faith alone is not enough. We have to go through the inner purging—which we may choose to do consciously, in the way this book has described the inner work, or which may also take place solely as the result of living and struggling and suffering and accepting, as has been the way for so many of our saints. Intellectual assent to a truth—in this case the

190

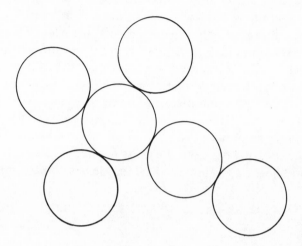

"I had a dream last year, when I was 51. It was really more of an inner picture while sleeping than a dream. I saw this large cross made of circles of colored glass or jewels—all different colors—lying down on its side. Then I woke up, and my heart was racing.

I knew what it meant right away. It was as if Jesus had said to me 'Lay down your cross. Let go. It's time to rest.' No, my life certainly isn't over—in fact, I feel as though it's really just beginning. And I certainly don't think I won't have problems or pains and suffering along the rest of the road; of course, I will. Everyone does.

But what it means to me is that I don't have to be fighting the fight, the war between the parts of myself. It's as though something bigger than me, inside me and outside too, is in charge—and whatever happens it will be all right. I've given up trying to make things happen that I think would be good for me or for others. Now, years ago I said this was how I felt, and that was true at the time . . . but now I can feel the difference, because I'm really living this way. It has just happened gradually. It is a sense of freedom from having to perform or achieve. The last time I felt that way was at about age 9.

Anyway, there was that very large and heavy cross laid down on its side to rest. And it's very beautiful; it has all the colors of the rainbow, and light shines through them. I hope that's how my life will be from now on."

truth of "I must die so that I may live"—doesn't equal being there (but it's as good a place as any to start).

When that Self-centeredness, that God-centeredness, is truly our way of being in the world, we are at home. . . at long, long last.

Sometimes the ego that has given away its primacy in the person is described as being like a clear lens; the light can shine through it. This person's light is colored with all the hues of the rainbow, that ancient symbol of the sacred marriage (or *hieros gamos*) between heaven and earth, spirit and matter. The richness of color comes from a half-century of living in twentieth century America and, many years ago, responding to the invitation to "take up your cross." Now, he can lay down the cross formed when two parts of us—ego and self—vie for inner rulership. He has come home.

Our tears shall all be wiped a-way
When we have ceased to roam,
And we shall hear our Mak-er say,
"Come, dwell with Me at home."

Not just about eternity, the beautiful song is also about what we can experience in *this* life when we seek first the kingdom of God.

Although many may not hear the call to growth we've been discussing in *Coming Home*, and it certainly isn't a call others can force upon them, there are many, many indications that more people than ever are experiencing and honoring this call. Here's what Thomas Merton wrote in 1971, shortly before his death:

" . . . whereas. . . psychological integration was, in the past, the privilege of a few, it is now becoming a need and aspiration of mankind as a whole."[2]

There are others who foresee a time—not too far distant—when people's natural urge toward wholeness will be much more known about and lived out than it is today. In the next chapter we will explore what C. G. Jung saw as the "new myth" of humankind, the search for consciousness. Jung spoke of "human heliotropism," the striving towards the light (literally, "turning to the sun," as plants do). Futurists who share their vision for the next millennium speak of children being exposed to the concept of their great possibilities from infancy on and taught the skills and attitudes to help actualize this greatness. The transformation of society could come about, it is hoped and prayed for by many, through the transformation of individuals. It will be, such visionaries believe, as though we each had a moral obligation to respond to our soul's inborn tendency to evolve . . . and shine forth.

A Map of the Soul: Our Soul-Scape

Let's take a look at this in a simple, visual way. Perhaps a picture of home—a geography of the soul, if you will—will help us discern our own closeness to or distance from the goal of the spiritual life. Is there a cartography of inner space, the way there are maps and star charts of the heavens and the outer cosmos?

We might start with the visual image of an actual house, as the journal exercises of the earlier pages of this book suggested. Will the picture of our own dream house be an adequate representation for us of that inner home? Here is one woman's report:

I call it home-cosmography.

—H.D. Thoreau

193

"*Back in the late '60's a favorite song of mine was Crosby, Stills, Nash and Young's Our House.[3] They sing about fresh flowers in a new vase, a newly-lit fire, evening sunlight shining through the windows like fiery gems:*

> *'Our house is a very, very, very fine house,*
> *With two cats in the yard,*
> *Life used to be so hard,*
> *Now everything is easy 'cause of you. . . .'*

and I could hear it as a song about God and myself. There was only one cat in my yard, but this cozy and undoubtedly white-picket-fenced house seemed to work for me as a description of a place inside.

Somehow, however, it seemed to be a little too concrete, a little too real. For instance, one day I found myself wondering if those shining windows were weatherstripped and how high the heating bill would be, and whether or not I would be able to continue finding firewood. All the practical home maintenance concerns kept popping into my idealized picture of the home inside."

Our best descriptions of real houses, while capturing the spirit of inner home in many ways, are somehow *too* concretized. They are *too* subject to outer necessity for most of us to see them as permanent images of that at-homeness that comes from life with our Maker. They aren't the best maps of the soul, although they are wonderful starting points in our attempts to describe something as ephemeral as the inner realm.

Let's look again, then, at the picture our Scriptural homes gave us, the image of the mandala. It is the diagram of perfection, with its sure center and its well-marked boundary, its sense of order and balance. Mandalas are a universal image which have been used by all peoples to represent their inner worlds. Here is C. G. Jung on the mandalic image; he drew his first mandalas while working as a doctor in the army during World War I, creating them quite spontaneously without knowing why:

> ". . . they seemed to me highly significant, and I guarded them like precious pearls. . . "

and in the 1950's, he was writing that

> "The basic motif (of a mandala) is the premonition of a center of personality . . . which is itself a source of energy. The energy of the central point is manifested in the almost irresistible compulsion and urge to *become what one is.* . . "[4]

Pear seeds grow into pear trees, nut seeds grow into nut trees, God seeds into God.

—*Meister Eckhart*

This urge to become what one already is was called by Jung "the religious instinct." Just as acorns grow into oaks and apple seeds into apple trees, we too have the imprint of our own wholeness embedded in us, and are (Jung's word) *driven* to make it become real. The psyche tends toward wholeness . . . and when we do not allow this, our life lacks peace and meaning. Jung speaks of his own beautiful mandalas, some of which can be seen in *C. G. Jung: Word and Image*, as "cryptograms concerning the state of. . . my whole being—actively at work."[5]

195

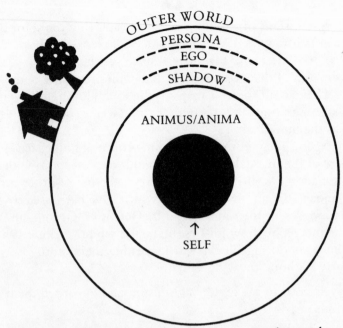

OUTER WORLD

PERSONA

EGO

SHADOW

ANIMUS/ANIMA

↑
SELF

Diagrammed in the simplest way, we can picture the soul this way:
The outer level is that of the ego, with its covering or *persona* and
its shadow layers, as yet unknown to us. These latter comprise
what we call the personal unconscious. Normally, this outer layer is
colored by the psychological energy that corresponds to one's
biological gender (masculine or feminine).

The middle layer of this onion-like soul is a deeper level of the
unconscious, and the most natural place for the contrasexual or
other-gender energy of the soul. In a woman, according to
traditional Jungian thought, it is the home of the *animus* or the
masculine components of her personality, and in a man, it is the
home of the *anima*, his feminine aspects. The animus or anima
functions in a two-fold way: it both mediates the life at the center
to the ego, and also supports the energies of the ego-layer of the
soul with their contrasexual complement. Without this latter
balance, either the feminine or the masculine rules the personality in
a lopsided adaptation.[6]

Finally, the image of God—the *imago Dei*—or the image known
as the Self lives at the center. . . as well as permeates through the
entire person. It is the true ruler of the soul-life. In psychology, we
can only speak of images. In religious language we speak of the
"the Christed Self, the God within." What we have here is an all-

too-simple picture of our personal mandala. For most people, it is unknown land, or what the early explorers called *terra incognita*.   The mandala is the map of the soul.[7]

See how accurately the Scriptural mandalas corresponded to the psychical one. At the center of this design is the very fixed, yet very alive, heart space representing That Which Is Unchanging, the Old Testament's "I am." In our Scriptural mandalas there was always something at the center to represent this permanent presence of the divine—the sacred trees, or the holy of holies or the ark, or the temple at the center of the city, or the Lamb on the throne. This was the precious, sacred centerpoint which enlivened the mandala and gave all else in the mandala its meaning. The same is true in our own inner world: it is the God living at our own center that gives our soul-life meaning. The revival of interest in centering prayer has helped many of us experience this sacred place as well as know about it. When we say we are "centered," it means this part of our being is in charge.

Around this still point, which is beyond time and space as we know them, are the sacred precincts or the protected space, the set-apart space. In the mandalic Holy City of *The Book of Revelation*, a beautiful crystal sea made from the waters of the river of life surrounds the image of God, the Lamb. It is like the waters of the unconscious, which cover most of our own soul-scape. Or, the soul is like a flourishing garden, or the interior of the temple.

And, finally, in our inner and our scriptural maps both, is the outer boundary line:

- the limits of the paradisaical garden

- the horizon lines or "as far as eye could see" of the promised land

- the walls of the temple

- the fortifications of the cities of both old and new Jerusalem

- the firmness of the healthy ego and its own sense of boundedness (an expression used for the *weak* ego by Jean Houston is that it has "leaky margins").

Here is Dr. Jung again:
  "I knew that in finding the mandala as an expression (of myself), I had attained what was for me the ultimate."[8]

"My idea of heaven is that I will have my home all in order. It seems as though I've fought a lifelong battle against clutter and dust, trying to get things shaped up, and I come from a long line of fanatical housekeepers. Our family has moved a lot, which has meant even more disorder and chaos in our living quarters, and when we remodeled and had to camp out in the yard I truly felt homesick.

Maybe this order can only come in another life. I wonder sometimes if the people who put together doll houses with expensive miniature furnishings all to scale, even down to the roll of toilet paper that unwinds, aren't striving for this home-perfection. Maybe that's one way we can get it in our homemaking. Certainly, those doll houses aren't for kids to play with. I just know that I love my home, and I want it to be perfect."

Down through the history of world religions, this pattern—the mandala—is repeated. We see it in the Christian tradition in

- rose windows

- beautiful icons, often of Mary with the Child in a circle at her own center

- baptistries of medieval and Renaissance times, separate from the churches and built in round or squared-off circle form (these often have beautiful mosaic mandalas on their ceilings)

- labyrinths in the floors of many of the European cathedrals of this period, winding passageways that stand for the pilgrimage of our lives

- even some feast-day foods (round Easter breads of the Mediterranean countries, for instance) and barn decorations of the Amish and other Pennsylvania German folk (what we call "hex signs").

Places of worship come in mandalic form in all religious traditions. Often they are squared-off circles, the squaring indicating symbolically that what is unseen or psychological or spiritual has been grounded and made conscious or manifest.[9] In the west we are used to oblong or cruciform churches, a legacy from the shape of the Roman basilica. But in the lands further to the east, including all of Asia, the shape of the place of worship is usually mandalic, as it is in so many primitive forms of religion.

The mandala has been most highly developed as a religious art form by the Tibetan Buddhists. Their temple and monastery floor plans are often mandalic in design, and they use intricate drawings and paintings called *thangkas* as a picture of their inner home.[10] In the center of the design is the holy kingdom with God, surrounded by walled gardens, often in layers. Gates, guarded by deities, lead inward. Some of the *thangkas* are filled with the inner beings one meets on the inward journey. We look at these beautiful works of art and hear the words of Jesus, "In my Father's house are many mansions."

The design of the mandala is universal, because it is God's motif. It is like the "logo of God," saying "the soul has coherence and meaning." The mandala is a map signifying the wholeness of creation, and representing the order beneath the apparent chaos of our lives. In fact, Jung and many others have noted that the internal design of the mandala often appears spontaneously in our lives—through our dreams, or even in as simple a thing as our doodling on a telephone pad—when we are under stress. At that time, the archetype of wholeness is constellated . . . because that is what the person needs. We most need the protective circle with its center in times of strife, a safe refuge from confusion and perplexity. It comes up from within like a "self-cure."

C. G. Jung said, "The archetype (of the mandala) . . . constellated represents a pattern of order which, like a psychological 'view-finder'. . . is superimposed on the psychic chaos so that each content falls into place and the weltering confusion is held together . . . "[11] The appearance of this pattern of our inner world reconnects us to the home within, and this is soothing and healing. The various fragmented pieces of our life get pulled back into the protective circle, and are given boundaries and a focal point. Order and harmony are touched once again, and we feel some peace. Many of us know this from our experience of turning to some sort of centering device (and the cross, especially the equilateral Greek cross, is such an image); teachers find that body centering or looking at a centering image can quiet down a whole classroom of students fresh from the playground.

The mandala is a picture of our inner universe, but also of the outer universe. Think of how it is repeated throughout creation, in

- the solar system (and its analog, the zodiac)

- pictures of far-away galaxies and nebulae

- the sun itself

- earth, our home—a spherical or three-dimensional mandala, with a central gravity point buried at its core.

In smaller ways, the mandalic pattern is found everywhere in God's created world, in

- a spider web

- the cross-section of a cell or of a tree trunk

The power of the world works in circles, and everything tries to be round.

—*Black Elk*

- flowers, opening to the sun from their heart-centers

- snowflakes

- crystals

- many trees, which—viewed from the top—open into perfectly centered designs.

All around us is this picture of perfect balance and symmetry. It is our Creator's own design, and we humans have manifested it for thousands of years; there are mandalic drawings some 30,000 years old. We look at cave drawings and find them; we find a picture of an ancient fortress or a pyramid in Egypt or Latin America, a city in ancient Britain or China . . . and there is the mandala, rising spontaneously from the soul of the simplest and most sophisticated peoples alike. They carved and erected and drew the image they knew best, and left it behind for us—-who carry within us that same image.

Closer to home, we can find a multitude of the same pattern:

- designs in rugs and wallpaper and tiles

- clocks and watches

- patchwork quilts and fabric motifs

- dishes and lids of pots and pans

- car steering wheels and dashboard dials

- baseball diamonds.

Many of these external and man-made mandalic forms have been created for functional reasons . . . and yet, once we begin to keep our eyes out for them, we cannot help but be amazed at how regularly the pattern pops up. The metapattern of the mandala lies hidden behind the busyness of our lives. It is the pattern of our souls, a self-portrait of each of us. We are living mirrors of the perfection of creation, containing the mandala within us. Oh yes, around it flow all the many outer aspects of our lives: our work, other people, our planet, groups and institutions—and each of these is influenced by the invisible image within each of us. The mandala is a picture of our soul-scape—it is the map of our true home.

"Behold now the Kingdom! See with new eyes!"

Owning Our Own Home

Long have I waited for your coming home to me, and living deeply our new life.

As mortgage rates climb and prices inflate, the long-dear dream of owning one's own home is just that—a dream—for a majority of people. Most of us and those who follow us will count ourselves fortunate to have a simple rented roof over our heads, at least for much of our lives.

Yet, taking to heart all that we've been exploring, it turns out that there is a home we can own. Not one of us need be homeless or alien. We've found that we carry our truest home within us, imprinted into our very nature. Once we have experienced it and its power, perhaps just in flashes or glimpses at first, we want to stay there. . . we want to own this home, not just taste it and then regress to our old way. We want to stay with God and live the new life we've spoken of, the life in which God, living in us, rules and flows through us. The ancient faiths tell us that this is the Lord's desire as well.

In this life we are never completely "home, at last." We never are finished, or individuated or self-actualized (to use the language of another of the great teachers about growth, Abraham Maslow). We are "finishing up," or "individuating," or "self- actualizing," or (Maslow's later language) "self transcending." The inward journey will only be done when we see God face to face . . . and will still go on, most likely.

The closest we come here on earth to inner-home ownership is when we can, *more* habitually than *not*, allow our lives to unfold, finding that we trust in the process and in the mandalic pattern of wholeness that is constantly striving for realization. Listen again to C. G. Jung, writing of the common denominator he perceived in his clients who grew beyond themselves (again the small s self):

> "Everyone must possess that higher level, at least in embryonic form. . . What did these people do (to grow beyond themselves)? As far as I could see they did nothing but let things happen. . . (but in most of us) consciousness is forever interfering, helping, correcting, and negating, and never leaving the simple growth of the psychic processes in peace."[12]

Jung is writing a commentary on an ancient Chinese text, and refers to a western equivalent of the letting-go of control he finds there: the teachings of Meister Eckhart, one of the thirteenth

century's Dominican school of mystics. He is describing the same experience as that had by our dreamer who finally found he could lay down his cross. When consciousness and unconsciousness are engaged in an inner struggle—or, "at cross purposes"—we are in exile. When the ego, our conscious vehicle, really says, "O.k., I am going to get out of the way and let the inner wisdom take over," we can lay down the cross. Then, the ego is available to the Self; it can take on the energy of whichever inner figure is needed at the moment—the hero, the mother, whoever.

This is the "at home" experience; the higher power is in charge of our lives when this happens. The perfection pictured in the mandala has a chance to come through, be revealed. It knows best, and will lead us—if we listen and respond. This is how we own our own home. . . hesitantly, at first, and then more surely, as we see the miracle of totality within coming to light. We just have to get out of our own way to see what's always been there.

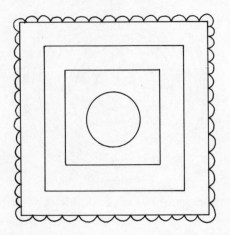

"I took my two little girls to the beach last week. It was so hot and sticky in the car going there, that I wondered if I shouldn't turn back and just let them play in the plastic pool in the back yard. We did go on, however, and when we got there, Sarah who is six headed straight for the water.

I stood at the edge of the ocean to keep an eye on her, for the waves were high and she would have really been wiped out if one had hit her very hard.

At the same time I had my other eye on Mary, my three year old. She had been just miserable all morning, whining and fussing, but now she was busy drawing in the damp sand where the tide had gone out.

I watched her make a series of squares, one around the other; they grew larger and larger, until she finally finished with a square about three feet on each side. I was surprised at how evenly spaced they were, for such a little girl. Then Mary started hunting for bits of shells and seaweed and she made a design around the outside of the largest square, like a wall.

She sat and looked at it for a while, and I asked her, 'Is it finished?' and she said, 'No, it needs one more thing.' For about five minutes she hunted around and then finally found what she was looking for, the lid from the circular box of potato chips we had brought for lunch. 'Can I have this, Mommy?' she asked me and, when I said she could, she took it and tiptoed between the lines she had made and put the silver circle down in the middle of her design.

The entire sand-drawing took her almost an hour to make, and for most of the rest of the day, she just sat near it, as calm as could be. I said to myself, 'Is this the little girl I was ready to throttle this morning?'"

Jungians sometimes use a sand tray and miniature figures in their practice to help people express themselves non-verbally, as little Mary did at the beach. There, in just this way, the mandala often appears, rising up from the depths of the unconscious—to restore order during times of fragmentation, to heal what has been broken, to picture for the sand-world-maker what might be. Frau Dora Kalff of Switzerland, pioneer of Sandplay in the Jungian mode, says the mandala appearing spontaneously in the sand is the starting point of a healthy ego development.[13]

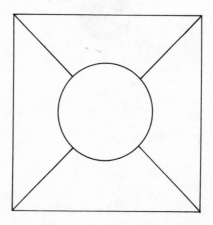

"Here is a dream I had, but first you need to know that all my life whenever I've doodled, this is the figure that has appeared:

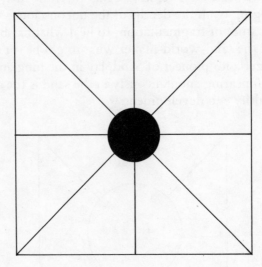

In my dream I am doodling this same shape. My friend looks over my shoulder and asks, 'Why are you doing this?' I respond that I don't know why I am doing it."

We may never own the estate on the hilltop or the condo in the singles building or the little house in the woods. The home within, however, is already ours, waiting to be claimed. We are all homeowners.

Personal Journal Pages
"Go, Rebuild My Temple"

Earlier, I designed my dream house (Chapter 3). How does this work for me as a picture of my soul? Have I internalized this image and found it prayer-producing or, perhaps, just peace-giving?

Now I can also allow the basic pattern of the Home of Homes within me—the mandala that is already there—to emerge. This is my truest self-portrait. Letting it be revealed is one way I can cooperate in God's ongoing creation. There are two complementary ways I can use to help uncover my own personal soul-picture:

1. Rest quietly, prayerfully. Allow the inner picture of totality to surface. This may take a good bit of time (days, years). It may be revealed during the night, in a dream; my soul-scape may come all at once, or in bits and pieces (which is more probable). On special paper used just for this purpose, I can let it flow out and draw it as I become more conscious of it.

2. Look back over the examples of mandalas in this book. There are scriptural patterns, centered designs from the world of nature, human-made centering devices. Which are most compelling to me? What clues do any of them give me about my own inner design? Can I now start to draw it, all the time listening to its presence in me?

A mandala has these three basic parts (and may have many additions and intricacies as well):

a. *The boundary*, of several possible shapes, such as

(The squared-off shapes indicate that the basic mandalic circle has been made more conscious, as noted earlier. When both square and circle are used—one inside the other—this is often seen as a symbol of the dialogue between the visible and invisible, the Incarnation or sacred marriage between earth and heaven, matter and spirit.)

The edges of the boundary are equidistant from

b. *The centerpoint*, which may also take several possible shapes, such as—

or which may be represented by some symbolic object or picture (remember, it is the center which represents God hidden in us). For example, one might use:

light	a fountain	a dwelling place
a jewel	a tree	a chalice
a well or spring	some image of God	a flower
an altar	the burning bush	the sun, a star

c. *The space within the boundary*, often divided up. It might, for instance, look like

a courtyard	a labyrinth
city streets	a wheel's spokes
many rooms or mansions	sections of a garden or parts of a forest

The God whose home this image is will let me know about it; I need not become rushed about getting it down on paper.[14]

There are ways I can use my personal mandala once I have drawn it. Here are some of them:

1. I can carry it with me in my heart, anywhere, any time. The mandala can always be present, and I can first be at one door or gate or side of it and then at another, or I might visit the One who lives at its core (if represented by a fountain, for example, I can go and be refreshed by the streams of living water), or I might some other times just be with it, resting at the still center. There are many possibilities of this sort of quiet, yet visual, prayer with the mandala. (The Jungian approach is, in general, very *kataphatic*, a word meaning that images are used as growth-catalysts.)

2. In a breathing meditation: while looking at the mandala

• with each inbreath, I ingest its symmetry and harmony.

• with each outbreath, I share the beauty and colors of my own soul-scape with the universe, especially that small portion of it which surrounds me. (In a sense, those who are *healers* are *living* mandalas; they radiate the harmony of their inner worlds to the rest of us.)

3. During stressful times, I can see myself enclosed by the mandala. Its boundaries can keep me from feeling invaded by negative energy that might come my way from other people or outer events, and if the stress comes from within, the balanced quality of the mandala will help to balance my emotions and body with its superimposed orderedness. It holds things together. When I reconnect with it, I reconnect with what most truly gives my life meaning—the inner home.[15]

4. When I am spending time engaged in any of my spiritual practices, I can relate them back to the mandala, so that they can be seen as pieces of a whole rather than as isolated exercises.

5. I might even draw or paint my mandala in an oversized form on some heavy material, so that when I need the centering of which it speaks, I can sit upon it in the mode of the native American Indians and their sand paintings.

6. I can hunt for music that fits my mandala and use it for prayer along with the visual picture. It might be *Rebuild My Temple* by John Michael Talbot,[16] or even the old *Building Up the Temple,* or some of the hymns about walking in the garden or traveling to the Holy City or Promised Land. It could well be songs or music

*If the Lord
does not build
the house,
then in vain
does the builder
labor.*

209

"I've had the children in my second grade class draw mandalas. I don't call them that, but just tell them to draw designs with a center that look 'even'—they instinctively know what to do, and have come up with some beautiful ones. The fifth-grade teacher down the hall has had her kids color the round paper lace doilies you get for parties and Valentines, then she mounts them on black paper.

Ours are up on the side bulletin board in our room. I've taught the children to look at their very own drawing when they feel upset or tired, and to focus especially on the center. One day I asked if they could describe what the centers of their pictures were like. Here are some of their answers:

- like the balancing place on the see-saw

- like a warm light. . . it shines

- like something moving, like water bubbling up

- like a heart beating

- a little voice inside me that doesn't talk

- like a smile that starts in the middle and spreads all through me

- a song in my heart.

Now I'm not a religious person at all, but these answers sound religious to me. Doesn't the Bible say something about a little child leading others? They are my teachers—sometimes I tell them that, and they all laugh."

about going home (the famous example being the *largo* or second movement from Dvorak's *Symphony from the New World* in E minor).

7. Simplest of all, if I just put my soul-picture up on a wall and live with it, it will speak to me of things deep inside—and remind me of the wholeness within me.

Around me there are other mandala-like designs. Here is some space where I can make notes about how I see four of the most common ingredients of my life as mirrors of my soul-picture:

• *The Place I Live In* (a SPACE MANDALA). Whether apartment in Hoboken or castle in Spain, each dwelling has its boundary, and can have its set-apart holy of holies (prayer corner, chair with a table for special things, garden shrine, family altar). At the center can be the representation of God. Going to that spot says "come back to Me . . . come home."

• *Each Day and Week and Month and Year of My Life* (TIME MANDALAS). Each twenty-four hours, each seven days, each block of thirty or thirty-one days, each set of twelve months can be seen as a circle that comes back to its starting point: a new morning, a new week, a new month, a new year. And while time does, indeed, march on, it also is a repetition of what has been. We usually view time in calendar or clock form, both of which emphasize time's passing. Here is another way to consider it, which makes it clear that all revolves around the present moment—which will be as God-filled (or empty of God) as we make it.

- *My Body* (a PHYSICAL MANDALA). The body has its enclosure—the skin—with its gates into the interior, and a physical center (which may differ from person to person, but is most often between the heart and the lower abdomen, the typical martial arts center). The body can be experienced as sacred space, as holy; Paul calls it a temple.

Earth's crammed with heaven and every common bush afire with God.

—Elizabeth Barrett Browning

- *The Primary Relationships in My Life* (a PERSON-TO-PERSON MANDALA). The most special relationships can be a container, too. Working from the outside in, the outermost layer can be seen as the sharing of day-to-day events that go on between the two people. Contained within this boundary comes sharing closer to home: feelings, touch, the excitement of shared work or play or ministry—all these things which bond people. At the core of friendship with a true soul partner is spiritual sharing: "God within me touches God within you." This is an intimacy reserved for the special few, a gift which must be two-way, not unilateral.

"Finding recreations of the mandala pattern in my outer world has really been helpful to me. I used to struggle so with trying to find time in my life for attending to the God within, but now 'how can I find the time?' has become a non-question. I have a very busy life as the rabbi of a large congregation in the midwest; I need to use what is outside to strengthen my consciousness of what is inside.

The word 'sacrament' is more of a Christian word, I believe, but the concept is certainly very Jewish. One of my favorite psychologists is Abraham Maslow, who uses the expression 'sacralization of life.' That's what we're talking about—living with the concept and the experience that what is without reflects what is within, and that there is no division between these two worlds, no polarizations, no chopped liver in the psyche.

Well, for me, some of the outer mandalas are easier to experience than others. The body is easy—I even see my clothes as part of the outer layer, and the area around my diaphragm as the center spot. Once I learned about centering prayer, finding God in that spot, it was as though I had to treat my body with more respect. I even gave up my precious pipe. And, in the sex education classes we have at the temple, we find that experiencing the body as sacred in this way is the best preventive education we could give to help our young people not treat their bodies and others' with disrespect. I hope they look at each other and see 'carriers of God.'

For a Jew, of course, the home as shrine with God at the center is a natural, and so is my relationship with my wife, the mother of my children. Our bondedness goes way beyond what we call 'romantic love'; we truly are one at our best moments.[17] It's harder to feel time in this way, but slowly I'm learning to stay in touch with the pulse of life, you might call it. There's the expression 'redeeming the time,' and seeing time as cyclic helps me to do this. Actually, both time and relationship turn out to be 'cyclic mandalic patterns,' and are intangible—and the body and where we live are very tangible mandalas, more static.

Well, this is how I use the outer mandalas that surround me as metaphors for the one that's hidden. They reinforce my awareness of my soul and its pattern. As I grow in doing this I see that the mandala is omnipresent. I have more 'unitive consciousness,' I believe it's called, just as small children do (but they don't know they have it). A Christian would, I should think, especially prize this approach because all of his or her faith is based on incarnation—Jesus coming in the flesh so people could know the invisible God. Sacramental living is something that binds people of all faiths, isn't it? Thanks be to God!"

CHAPTER EIGHT

A Picture of the Homebody

The Shiny Person

We need to spend a little more time looking at the qualities of the person who is "at home." (Chapter Six gave us a start, describing images of the Self.) We might call him or her a real homebody. Our last chapter gave us the major characteristics of this person:

The person who has journeyed and is close to home or at home, is one who is no longer trying to make things happen.

This person has learned to trust in the process of growth that is already under way, knowing that God is as much in charge of his or her unfolding as that of the acorn's or the rosebud's or the baby sparrow. He or she *really* means, "Thy will be done."

Though strong in a sense of self, the homebody we're speaking of *feels* (as well as knows) the higher Self as the central point of his or her being. . . and rejoices in this.

This person is living in union with God. . . more often than not.

The religions of the world have long had language for such people. They are called saints. How quickly we back away from that word! Yet, it was the language of the gospels and of Paul, who addressed his fellow believers as "saints." The world once simply

Consider the lilies: they neither toil nor spin.

215

meant those who had their hearts fixed on God, on their true home—first on this earth and then after death. Today, we invest it with all sorts of stuffy overtones and trappings of self-denial and suffering. . . and, yet, the common denominator of the saints was that they were filled with joy! They were happy because they knew what their lives were about. . . loving, and being loved by God and others.

Perhaps we would do better to describe the saints with images. The one used most often, from east to west and north to south, is *light*.

"You are the light of the world," the one who "shall light up as the brightness of the firmament, . . . as stars for all eternity,"[1] read the Scriptures. Various traditions speak of the person who is "enlightened," or "illuminated," or "transparent" or "clear"; this is the person who allows the light within—God's life at his or her center—to shine forth. We sing about such persons and are shown the way by their light, warmed and energized by it. They show us what we, at our best, might become.

Our pictures of these light-bearers show them with halos or auras—light surrounds them. Moses' face shone, and he did not

Joy is the infallible sign of the presence of God.

—*Léon Bloy*

Good people
shine from afar,
like the Himalayas.

know it. Jesus, at his shiniest, is called by us the *glorified* Christ after
the Resurrection and, earlier, the *transfigured* Christ. In both
phrases, we feel light and brightness. The white garments of Easter,
for the newly baptized or (in a diminished version) as new Easter
clothes, are about this inner light as well. In Tibet, the diamond is
pictured at the center of the person, shining out.

Conversely, we describe someone without the inner light as
"grey," or "burnt out." Earlier, in Chapter Four, we spoke of fairy
tale images of the person whose ego had hardened into a shell, or
who had been turned to stone, or locked in a tower. The ending of
such stories is often an emergence of the light, bright person inside.
The princes (traditionally shiny people, along with princesses, kings
and queens) who are first met in beast guise or frog skin or feathers
of swans evolve during their tales and end up as the most beautiful
of men. Cinderella, whom we first meet among the ashes,
metamorphoses into a delicate and light-filled belle of the ball,
wearing "a gown of gold and silver, beset with jewels," according
to an early version of the story. Her slippers are of glass, sparkling
in the candlelight. She radiates. Fairy tales, which often are parallel
versions of legends of the saints, are filled with people who struggle
and journey, and end by being shiny people. They stand for us—
garden-variety saints who can do the same.

"Do you know the story of The Snow Queen?

I remember reading it to my son and daughter when they were about seven and eight, in a shortened form of the long Hans Christian Andersen version. That was a couple of years ago. It gave me shivers, because I was reading to them about myself—although, of course, I didn't say so.

Briefly, the story's main location is in the frozen kingdom of the Snow Queen, whose kiss is colder than ice. . . and brings death. The hero, a boy named Kay, is taken off by the queen; his heart—the center of his being—has turned into a lump of ice. Up until this time he had thought well of himself, but in the presence of the Snow Queen he always feels lacking. Kay's days are spent asleep, at the feet of the Snow Queen.

This royal ice woman presides over her kingdom from a frozen lake, all broken up, which is called 'The Mirror of Reason.'

Kay doesn't even realize he has lost the life he once lived, a life with little Gerda, the girl next door, and his parents and grandmother. He spends his time in the Snow Queen's dark, winter kingdom forming words out of ice, all the time having the one most important word elude him. This is the word Eternity.

Here I was, a pretty successful used car salesman living in Cleveland in the 1970's. When it snows here, we have warm indoor heating to turn to and fireplaces to light. Still, reading to my children I felt so much like the hero of this story that it sent a chill down my back. I know what it's like to be frozen and in cold storage. It feels as though no one can get close to you, and you can't get close to anyone. It feels as though you have a thick layer over your heart, and that the iceman you've turned into covers up all that's good inside you.

I was glad my son and daughter had gotten sleepy by the time I reached the end of the story, so they couldn't hear the pain in my voice. The story ends with Gerda, the little girl, loving Kay enough to travel to the ice palace and free him with her love. They travel back home together, where birds are singing and roses are in full bloom . . . and where it is summertime again.

How can I get thawed out? What kind of love can I hope for in my life that will melt the hard shell of ice I've built up for forty years?—or do those things only happen in fairy tales?"

No, those things don't only happen in fairy tales. The shininess
in this man may be covered over and frozen away now, but all
we've been exploring so far leads us to the conviction that it is
there, that he too can undergo transformation. What transforms is
the fire of love, which may come from without—as in the story, or
from within—as the indwelling God of love flickers up and then is
tended to, carefully, and allowed to blaze. This warmth is what
melts and breaks up the light-concealing layers of ice—or
egocentricity, to go back to our psychological language.

And, as the layers melt, the dark icy stillness of winter in such a
person's heart begins to be replaced by the light and warmth of
spring. The person becomes more transparent, his frigidity replaced
by the inner light, now visible. That light becomes the most
important thing of all to him, and the most noticeable of his
qualities to others. No longer frozen and rigid, he shows to others
the brightness of his new center, the living flame of love at his very
core. Like the saints in our stained glass windows he—or she—will
have become a shiny person.

The winter is over and done.

In *The Creation of Consciousness*, Jungian analyst Edward Edinger
of Los Angeles elaborates on the shiny person. He sees each of us as
having the task of "collecting the sparks of God's life loosed on the
earth" and, citing Jung, postulates this work as the new myth that
will give meaning to people of a new age. He builds on the ancient
gnostic and Jewish idea of the *scintillae* or "the glory," an idea kept
alive down through the ages by people of diverse traditions. We
find it in Greek mythology, as Danaë is showered by flickering
gold from Zeus and becomes pregnant with the hero Perseus. In the
first century of Christianity, there were those who tried to connect
with the shining sparks in "the ensouled world" all around them
(even to the extent, Dr. Edinger reports, of spending much time
eating *melons*—cantaloupes and other golden fruit—in an attempt to
ingest what looked like shininess to them!).

In the Renaissance, we meet the same idea in the mystical Jewish
Hasidic tradition, particularly in the school of Isaac Luria of Safed
in Galilee. Meister Eckhart had spoken of this concept earlier: "the
little soul-spark." We find the same thought in alchemy, and in
fairy tales handed down by oral tradition (see, for instance,
Grimm's fairy tale number 24, "Mother Holle" and its variants, in
which the good daughter of a widow releases a shower of gold/
precious gems whenever she speaks). Those familiar with yogic

language will see the parallel to the Indian concept of *prana*.

The beautiful transcultural image of the sparks of God loose in the world persists in our day: theologian Monika Hellwig uses the expression "the face of God among us," and viewers of *Star Trek* have on the screen the visual image of this idea, as the crew of the *Enterprise* is continually "energized"—and broken down into shining bits of matter.

For Jung and for Edinger, this life of God which we are here to re-gather translates into consciousness—not just for the sake of personal growth, but also for the purpose of averting the destruction of our earth through *unconsciousness*. Translating the same idea to religious settings, we see that if it is unconsciousness which perpetuates such things as sexism and clericalism in institutional religion, it will be the re-collecting of consciousness by the people of God that is our best hope for changing these evils.

So, we see that the ideal of "the shiny person" has many sources and also has a direct tie-in to analytical psychology. Using this point of view, we can say that our growth in faith and prayer—that is, our continuing conversion—can be measured by our increasing consciousness and awareness of the presence of God's life within us, and within all about us. We also call this "sacramental living," using the broadest concept of the word "sacrament." It is an old idea, yes, but also excitingly new and of the future. It says that all of us have the possibility of becoming shiny people.[2]

Let your light shine.

"I had this dream:
'There are three short red candles.
On them are written the words YOU and YOUR.'"

"You Have Made Us Little Less Than the Angels"

The world's religions share, in common, a special light-filled sort of creature: the angel. There are, of course, the beautiful Christian angels—singing *glorias* at Christmas over Bethlehem and, earlier, Gabriel announcing to Mary the coming of her son. Angels minister to Jesus: on the mount of temptation, in Gethsemane. An angel is at the tomb on Easter morning, "his countenance like lightning, his garments like snow." The Hebrew scriptures too have angels: the angel of death passing over Egypt and Raphael, who walks with Tobit, to mention only two.

The religious traditions of the near and far east are equally as angel-populated; there are dark-haired, dark-eyed angels of Islam, guiding the prophet Mohammed, and angels of India and China dressed in native garb and watching over the peoples of those countries. In Africa, there is a tradition of black angels, and in ancient Egypt and Assyria, winged guardians of mighty power.

The angel is a universal and beloved image, just like the home. And the angel is connected with home in more ways than one— sometimes as guardian, more often as a resident of the kingdom of heaven. Yet, this is the kingdom that, we keep reminding ourselves, is already here, within us. The angels are the ultimate in shiny people. Yes, people—even though traditional angelology tells us they are spirit beings, we have personalized and enfleshed and named the angels, and the word itself is used over and again for *human* people.

"You're an angel," we say. (The word has special meaning in the theatre as someone who is the backer of a show.) Thomas Aquinas is called "Angelic Doctor" and the supreme painter of shiny people, Fra Angelico. There are the songs: old ones that speak about *Teen Angel* and *I Married an Angel*. These are about mortals, not winged creatures; the word has bridged heaven and earth, just like Jacob's angel-filled ladder. And we recall that the Judaeo-Christian tradition has taught us we are made "little less than the angels." The Muslims take it further, speaking of humans as "terrestrial angels"—earth angels, we would say.[3]

We have been looking for images that will describe the person who is becoming perfected. Having a picture of what we might, potentially, become gives us a standard or a touchstone that words like "holiness" or "individuation" do not. The angel, being of light, seemed at first to be a supernatural creature, but—perhaps— may be just that personal image or picture we need. True, most of us probably never will become angelic, yet it is good to have some idea of what we might be at our shiniest.

Let's take a look at angel qualities, as described in a number of cultures. Will they help us know better who we were born to become?

The word "angel" suggests many things to us. We imagine them

- with large, swift wings that make a rushing sound

- as messengers

- as guardians—of people, places, entire nations

- making music and dancing and singing

- involved in judgment

- praising God

The angels of the many choirs of heaven have, it seems, a variety of qualities and tasks. They are multi-purpose beings, and when we take time to explore their lore it becomes clear to us that they actually have what seem to be contradictory qualities.

Throughout this book we've been coming across an interesting phenomenon: things seemingly opposite can co-exist—and this co-existence, or harmonizing of pairs of opposites is a higher state of being, a better way, than "either/or" sort of living. With our human short-sightedness, we tend to chop things up into compartments:

- the outer world and the inner world

- human and divine

- matter and spirit

- masculine and feminine. . . and so many other pairs.

The wise . . .
set an example
to all.
Not putting on
a display,
they shine forth

—Tao Te Ching

There is truth in these dichotomies, of course, and they serve a purpose at a certain stage of our development. The higher truth, however, is that we are able to be inclusive enough to embrace

222

these and other pairs of complements, claiming them all as part of our nature. "Both _____ and _____" is a richer way of living than "either _____ or _____."[4] One of the famous lines from the apocryphal *Gospel According to Thomas* is

". . . when the inner and the outer are one, and the above is like the below, and the male and the female one and the same. . . then you will enter the kingdom."[5]

So, the person who is living in the kingdom (or, in the primary image of our book, the one who is at home) will be one in which the various complements are in harmony or balance. To use C. G. Jung's language: "All the possibilities of life are conserved."[6] This person has a more unitive life; it is easy to see why—the person at home is living closely united to God, and it is the nature of God to contain all things, not just part of the creation.

The angels, according to the lore of the ages, are just such paradoxical beings. They contain many pairs of opposites. For example, we discover that they not only

- shine luminously, but also have a dark side (there are the fallen angels, who show us the angelic shadow nature);

- are citizens of heaven, but also are intimately involved in the affairs of earth (again, the *hieros gamos* or sacred marriage);

- are peaceful and serene, as shown by their lovely faces, but also are strong warriors, able and willing to do battle when necessary (some wear armor and brandish swords for this very purpose);

- are gentle and compassionate, but also firm and just, able to mete out justice and help weigh souls;

- are able to rejoice and know heavenly bliss, but also experience earthly anguish—they have a full range of emotions;

- are innocent, simple and childlike (and are even shown in miniature or as babies, sometimes, to emphasize these qualities), but also are infinitely wise, so much so that they can serve as our guides and teachers. They seem to be both playful and serious, ever-young as well as eternally mature (actually, they are ageless).

- are good with words—the angels are winged ambassadors, announcing tidings of great joy and carrying messages all over the place, but at the same time are fluent in what we would call right-brain activities: making music, singing, painting pictures, dancing. (Apparently, they also know when to keep silent; it is said that even their wings make no noise in flight.)

- are usually masculine in their stature and strength (and names), but also feminine in their features and grace. They are, in fact, androgynous beings, combining the qualities of both genders.

- have a permanent home base, but also a tremendous amount of freedom;

- are able to travel alone, be content with themselves, but are also big on community: many of them live in choirs and interact in harmony;

- are much like each other, with their human forms and mighty wings, but also are (according to the artists of the world) each uniquely individual. No two sets of feathered wings seem to be the same in God's wonderful angelic creation.

So, the angels, combining within their nature pairs of opposites, can be a sign to us of that higher way of life. For we, too

- have both darkness and the light within us

- live both in heaven and on earth, are immortal yet mortal, can be in this world but not of it

- can be peacemakers and, at the same time, fighters for justice

- have a full range of emotions available to us

- have times both of extraversion and introversion, involvement in the outer world and attentiveness to the silent inner world

- can be wise as serpents, but simple as doves

- are at our best when androgynous

- need both intimacy and solitude in our lives

- can be free, even while having a fixed base of operation

- are bonded to others by our likeness to them—but also are absolutely unique, each called by name

224

• are at our best when we are using as many facets of ourselves as possible, not just our thinking or our feeling or our sensing or our intuiting.

The angels come from the east and the west and the north and the south. The diverse parts of ourselves, the people Jesus speaks of in Luke 11:29, will come from the east and west and north and south too, and they will all sit down at the feast in the kingdom of God. As we grow, there will be a balancing of these opposites within us, a richness of personality that will unfold as the image of shining wholeness that has always been there is uncovered.

"Everything living dreams of individuation, for everything strives toward its own wholeness," says Jung.[7] The manifestation of this wholeness, this balancing out of the opposites, is not without its pain, certainly; our own egocentricity will wrestle with the Self for primacy just as Jacob wrestled with his angel and was wounded by it. Yet, as the person becomes more holy, the seeming opposites of ego and Self, or human and divine, will also live more in harmony with each other. It is then that we shine brightly, like the angelic ones. This is not the same sort of thinking that once raged through Christianity in the form of assorted gnostic heresies (as Manichaeism, Catharism, and many other –isms). These dualistic approaches to life would have had us turn into celestial angels and leave matter behind. Our valuing of the angel is as a symbol—a powerful symbol completely foreign to gnosticism. For us, the angel is a symbol of the union of opposites rather than the separation of them.[8]

Theologians may argue over the existence of angels and their nature (how many, really, *can* dance on the head of a pin?). Psychologically, such arguments miss the point. The reason we have such a legacy of angels is because the archetype of Angel lives within each of us. If they were not within, we could not imagine them without. When the angels are met as larger-than-life images common to the souls of all peoples, we see them as a sign of what we too might become: beings of light, beings filled with confidence, beings of love and harmony and totality. This is a good picture of the person who has come home.

Wings

One feature of the angels, their most outstanding feature, deserves just a little more of our time. This is their beautiful, powerful feathered wings. Some angels have many pairs of rustling wings, it is written, and some have eyes in each of the feathers of their wings . . . the better to see (or, become conscious). Wingedness has a symbolism all its own, which will give us yet another way of describing this homebody person we are called to become.

Since the earliest recorded history, we know that humans have envied the birds their ability to rise above the earth, to get higher up, closer to what seemed to be God's realm. . . because for all peoples the heavens have traditionally been "up." The prophet writes, and we sing today that God

> ". . . will raise you up on eagle wings . . . make you to shine like the sun . . . "[9] (if we trust in the Lord)

The psalmist expresses the same longing for the transcendence of everyday life's limitations as the wish for

> ". . . the wings of a dove, that would take me far away . . ."[10]

Humans have tried to fly.

- Primitive peoples have attached feathered wings to themselves, the best known being Icarus, who flew so near the sun that the wax glue holding his feathers melted and he plunged into the sea. (The Icarus story is about *hubris*, or the inflated attempt to force one's way into higher, spiritual energies without the necessary initiation and purgation. Many of us know about trying to fly too soon.)

- Dervishes twirl in Arab nations, and Shakers whirled in their communities a century ago, using their flight-like spinning sacred dance to remove them from ordinary consciousness and get to that state which is "other"; even small children do this regularly, in an attempt to achieve an altered state of consciousness different from their mundane way of being.

226

- We fly planes and hang glide and sky-dive, even fantasize rides on magic carpets or winged horses, all to capture the sense of freedom and closeness to the heavens which is so beautifully expressed by the bird.

It seems that wingedness goes not only with angels—those idealized forms of what we might become—but has been used throughout history in connection with human beings who are, somehow, trying to go beyond their earthly or most familiar state. And there are many examples of people who have been given wings or flying power as a symbol of their ability to transcend:

- Colonial tombstones abound throughout our country with winged beings engraved upon them. At first, we might assume these are angels, then learn that they are pictures of the deceased, who has "taken flight" to a better world.

- We are familiar with the emblems of the four evangelists, each with its wings. These say that their writing about Jesus was a message from a higher world, from which one can look down and see a more total picture than is possible from an earthly perspective.

- Origen tells us that Melchizedek became an angel—that is, a larger-than-life being; the Dominican preacher St. Vincent Ferrer is often pictured with wings.

- Our superheroes can usually fly, or at least leap tall buildings with a single bound. Again, the message is "the person who has gone beyond humdrum, everyday life can rise above."

- The alchemists of medieval and later times pictured the androgynous person, one who had gone through the sort of transformation this book is about, as a winged being, and the

227

alchemical guide invariably was winged as well, as befits the one who leads a procession through the psyche. (C. G. Jung drew a picture of his wise inner guide, a bearded man named Philemon, with wings.)

• Shamans of primitive cultures have often attached wings to themselves or dressed as birds, to stress their other-worldliness and transcendent abilities. Jung wrote, too, about the going-up that wings symbolize. He said problems often are not solved, but outgrown. The thunderstorms may still rage on in the valley, but we can go higher up the mountain and see a problem from above, with a broader perspective. That way, we are no longer in the thunderstorm, but above it.[11] (Or, even if we still get drenched, we also have a higher consciousness at the same time.)

Going up is the vantage point of the person with wings, the one who is little less than the angels. For Christians, the ascension of Jesus and the assumption of Mary are other images of this exaltation of human nature. No, of course, we will never *be* angels, even earth angels, any more than we will *completely* live in our own inner home (though there is a tantalizing legend that the thrones of the fallen angels are reserved for the saints).[12] More often, probably, we will feel our wings are somewhat clipped.

The angel and the home and the shiny person are the ultimates, the visions, the transcendental signs. It is good for us to carry them in our hearts. They tell us that *we* will be

• light-filled with the brilliance of the God of Love,

• channels of creativity, as the energy once used to maintain ego-dominance becomes freed,

• able to operate from a broader and peace-filled overview,

when
  we are
    home
      at last.

"Over the years I've worked out what I call a 'walking meditation' (because you don't have to go off and sit down to do it). First, I get in touch with my center, where I imagine there is a small spark. I think of the rest of me like a house or temple that contains this light—which is an exciting idea when you think about it.

Then, I remember that all the world around me is filled with more of this same kind of spark. . . and the spark in me can connect with the sparks around me. For example, the people I work with at the bank each have the same kind of light in them, even if they don't know it. When I'm standing next to Cecelia (she's the teller at the accounts receivable window next to mine), I can sense a link between the flicker in her and the one in me. There's almost a flow between us—I absorb the light she sends out and, in turn, send her back some of my light. It's like breathing in and breathing out.

I try to do the same thing with the customers who come to my window too, but it's interesting to see how many there are who are so boxed-off you can't get close to them. . . it's as though they were behind a wall or something. With them I just try to send the light out. Or, if you get people who are angry and sending all kinds of negative energy your way, sometimes the best you can do is set up a protective shield around yourself so you don't absorb their bad vibes. I'd like to learn how to turn it around so they feel better—but that's really high level stuff, and I'm just a beginner at this.

Now, I've found that there are all sorts of things around that I can 'feed on,' if you know what I mean. It's as though I'm living in an ocean of minute sparkles, always ready for me to soak in . . . they're in nature, in music, in plants and animals and pictures I have in my room, in the air, everywhere. I can almost feel them. They seem to collect at my center, but they flow all through me too.

I think the best thing about trying to live tuned in to the energy all around me is that it makes everything so alive, and every day sort of exciting. You never know what's going to come your way next to recharge you, so you find that you're—how can I say it?—well, living expectantly, waiting for the next surprise. And these can come from outside, such as when you meet someone really sparkly, or from inside when things just rise up in you—like a great idea, or a fantastic dream, or knowing that God's there and being able to pray.

The more I practice this way of being, the more light I have to send out and share. I'm really getting happier all the time; sometimes I feel as though I'm soaring. Yes, there are days I forget all about this and there have been times of trouble that wipe me out . . . but I keep coming back to this. And, you should see how my plants are growing, especially the Boston fern next to my bed!"

MAY THE FORCE BE WITH YOU

Personal Journal Pages

Times I've Taken Wing

- Here is space for my memories of times I've been at my best—my most light-filled, angelic (in the sense of being balanced) self. These flashes of how I can really be give me a glimpse of what might be ahead for me. (Important: I mustn't overlook childhood times that illustrate this freer me; the goal of spiritual growth is the becoming again like little children—but in a conscious way. Getting in touch with my childhood experiences of union with creation can help me recognize this experience when it comes again.)

And, following, are pages to continue this record. By dating my entries, I can see if the frequency of such experiences is increasing.

Here are some words different people have used to describe their better times. These are the at-home feelings. Which are typical of the special "best self" times I've listed above?

unrushed
calm
deep peacefulness
flowing
spontaneous
centered
quieter
creative
self-accepting
braver
excited about life
a channel
less controlling
not needing to
  be needed
enjoying the
  small things
more realistic in
  my expectations
more desire for play

simplicity
letting go
not striving
attentive
expectant
confident
empathic
happy
less easily unwired
in the right place
less self-conscious
less needing others'
  approval
less critical
energetic
better able to
  see beauty
spending my
  time more
  intentionally
my sense of humor flows

time to appreciate
balanced
being
anonymous
oneness
trusting
accepting
self-nourishing
contented
loving
never bored
need less outside
  stimulation
less judgmental
very present to what
  is happing *now*
failures/mistakes/criticism
  seen as a way
  to learn,
  not as a threat

What other words would I add, based on my experiences?

Have I ever been sent—in a dream, or from without—a shiny person that might be something like me at my best? (For some, it is an angelic being, for others some sort of super-person, or a royal figure. Look for someone of the same gender, or an androgynous being.) This is a Self-image, the image of God or *imago Dei* or Christed Self which is to be the ruling center of my soul.

How can I make use of this image and let it speak to me today?

When reading the works of C. G. Jung and his followers, I might come away with the impression that individuation is only for the few—the fortunate few who are either terribly blessed with grace or with enough money to afford individual analysis. Yet, Jung himself wrote over and over about the urge to wholeness within *everyone*, and believers have difficulty with the idea of "an elect," the elitist few (especially when we reflect on the everyday sorts of people to whom Jesus was attracted).

Here are two spaces for reflection that may help reconcile these seemingly opposing points of view:

• Jung was a man of the first half of the twentieth century, primarily (his dates are 1875 to 1961). He was in on the foundation-laying of this century's own science, psychology, and was a grown man and the father of five children *before* the outbreak of World War I. By the time of World War II, he was in his mid-sixties, a "senior citizen" who would not live to see the opening of the second Vatican Council. All of his life was lived in Switzerland, although he traveled widely. Jung's work so transcends time and location that we may tend to overlook his historical and geographical rootedness, which did affect his universal approach.

What books, articles, films or television shows have I read or seen that can help me get the feel of C. G. Jung's times? What is my sense of comfortable life in early and mid-twentieth century Europe? What, especially, are the qualities of that civilization that make it *different from* today's world (especially life in the United States)?

• What is there in my culture today that makes the ideas of spiritual growth/sanctity/individuation *more accessible to the many* than they would have been in early and mid-century Europe? (Some clues: the human potential movement and its popularization through the media; the lyrics of popular songs since the sixties that often refer to transpersonal values; the even greater need today for consciousness [the life of our planet is at stake]; the democratic ideology of American life, particularly, that assumes "good things" are potentially accessible to everyone; evidences of spiritual hunger; increased leisure time in more people's lives.) Here are specific examples:

(See the dream of C. G. Jung described in the introduction to *Man and His Symbols*, the book he organized in his mid-eighties. At the end of his life, he too was broadening his vision of just who was called to the individuation process.)

CHAPTER NINE

Enjoying Our Home

The House Built Upon Rock

Our book has been about a lifelong adventure, one that makes life really worth living. Jesus spoke of it this way:

> "There was a wise person who built a house upon rock. And the rain fell, and the floods came, and the winds blew and beat against that house, but it did not fall because it was founded on rock."[1]

For people who own a home, it is almost always their single largest lifetime investment. Once it becomes theirs, it doesn't maintain itself—but requires attention and investment of time and money and energy (there's always a leaky faucet or a cracked wall to be repaired). When payments are not kept up, a home can be lost. A home really owns its inhabitants, it is a demanding possession—yet, people still sacrifice and work and save to have a home of their own. It is worth the care and effort. The sense of security and rootedness and belonging that a home engenders are what make the expenditures worthwhile.

Just as this is true on an outward level, so it is also true inwardly. We may eagerly embrace the idea and initial experiences of inner home, then find that taking care of that space requires an investment of time and energy that conflicts with the rest of our lives. The inner home demands that we rearrange our priorities to take care of it; the comfort it offers calls us to do that rearranging so we can enjoy our inner home. For those who have glimpsed the hidden treasure of the inner kingdom the rearranging is done because it *must* be done. (Jesus' examples are of not looking back once we put our hand to the plow, and of finishing the tower once we begin to build it.)

We are called to continue to do the things that will assure an inner home built on rock, not sand. We don't want to lose it.

"If I forget you, O Jerusalem,
May my right hand be forgotten!
May I never be able to sing again
If I remember you not,
If I do not think of you as my greatest joy."[2]

Can we forget our own Jerusalem? Is it possible to have tasted the delights of life in the kingdom, to have caught a glimpse of home—or actually lived there—and then forget this experience?

This can happen; it does happen. We lose sight of what's most important, and disconnect from our most recently won consciousness. We are called to life in the kingdom, and that life requires a fixedness of purpose, a singleheartedness. The scriptures remind us of the opposite — the person with the divided heart:

I am in the middle of a regressio

"Not long ago I was reviewing my journals of several years past. I realize now that when I was in my mid-40's and had just become a therapist and consultant I was going through a severe inner crisis, which I only later understood to be a bad case of burnout.

For me consciousness has always been like an island, and our spiritual task is to lower the water line around the island by pulling up the contents of the deep. During this burnout time, it's as though the water line rose to such a height that I was almost submerged by it. My island's size really shrunk. At that time, I felt as though I had regressed back to a very immature stage of my life spiritually . . . now I realize that the dark, crisis periods are also times of growth. The expression 'dark night of the soul' always used to seemed like mystical poetry; now, however, I realize that I have experienced it firsthand.

Rereading my journal from those years, it's interesting to me now to see that what got waterlogged and resubmerged was my most newly acquired consciousness at that time. Let me explain: for me, sensation is what's called my 'inferior function,' the one of the four least developed in me.[3] In my late 30's I felt I had really made some headway in strengthening this function through drawing and working in clay, and focusing exercises while driving (such as 'there is a red car on my right' and 'I am going two miles over the speed limit').

Seven years later however, my journal tells me that this awareness had slipped away: my calendaring was a mess—I had double-booked appointments all the time, my weight went up fifteen pounds because I would eat without thinking or even tasting what went in my mouth, and—would you believe?—within a period of three months I drove away from gas pumps three times with the gas hose still in my car (each time ripping the hose out of its socket). Talk about the absent-minded professor! As C. G. Jung would have said, 'The problem with the unconscious is that it is unconscious!'

Now I've started doing, again, the things I have to do to catch my elusive sensation function—it's like the fish that keeps slipping off the hook."

"I know your works; you are neither cold nor hot . . . because you are lukewarm . . . I am about to vomit you out of my mouth."[4]

Strong words! This is one of those passages we like to slip by, for it sounds more like the destroyer of Sodom and Gomorrah than the God of love, who invites us to "set me as a seal on your heart." The Creator is saying we have no choice but to continue to give primacy in our lives to the innermost dwelling place. When we can do that—or, better still, when we can get out of the way (ego) and allow the inner home (God/Self) to run things—we will be living as we are designed to live. The person who has transited from self-centered living to Self- (or God-) centered living is like the person who sold all in order to purchase the field with the hidden treasure. It keeps getting back to priorities, doesn't it?

Fence-straddling or waffling or lukewarmness is hard. When we finally commit to the call to stay at home—stay with God—the "home maintenance chores" become not chores, but a joy. Just as planting a garden or decorating for the holidays or cleaning out a drawer can be peaceful and nourishing activity in an outer home we love, so too can the giving of our best time to prayer and dream logging and all the things of the inner life be a joy, once we are committed to that life. They will be done out of love; they make a home our own, just as the tasks of outer homemaking do.

Yes, when we first find a home, there are an enormous amount of tasks at hand: in the outer home, all the chaos of moving in, the fixing up and redecorating and shopping that's necessary—and, in the inner home, the learning of how to recall dreams, the experimenting with many different ways of prayer, the reappreciating of our religious heritage and roots, perhaps the search for a prayer partner or support group or spiritual guide. But this initial time of shifting doesn't last. . . fortunately!

There comes a time when things are more in order. In the outer home, we have finally arranged the furniture to our liking, and the garden is planted, and the garage shelves are (at last) cleared of old paint cans and rusty nails. In the inner home, we also get to a plateau time, a time when we have learned the skills of the inner life, have a working familiarity with its language (the language of symbols and image), no longer are struggling between the call to inner growth and the busy demands of our lives.

We learn to simplify. Spiritual practices don't have to be complex and convoluted; we learn that quality is preferable to quantity. We find we don't need to multiply prayers, or spend endless hours with our journals. Instead, all things having their season, we find there are times when we are called to focus intently on our dreams, and other times when our primary spiritual practice will be just the quiet awareness of the presence of God. That, we hope, will stay and then we find we've been sent two or three days just for attentiveness to a new symbol that has risen up from within. . . and so we go back to the journal and our art supplies. Next may come a period of intensive study, or appreciation of the liturgy, or perhaps playing an instrument and singing songs that spring up

My definition of home: "There, where life resounds, a clear pure note in the silence."

—Dag Hammarskjöld

from our centermost place. These things don't have to be done all at once, but may each have its time—just as, once settled in an outer home, we wouldn't try to add on a new room, replant the garden and throw a wedding reception for two hundred guests all in one summer. There will also be inner vacation times when we read nothing heavier than the sports pages, to give the soul-life a breather. "To everything there is a season . . . ," in the spiritual home as well as the material.

The best part of the inner home-ownership is that we don't have to make the decisions about what to focus on at any one time. The co-habitant of that home, the Lord, is really in charge of the process. We can't control it; our stance is that of the listener, the spiritual detective, watching and waiting for the clues about what the true Guide would have us attend to now. We are sent what we need. The ruling energy of our soul is the God dwelling at its very core, not our own limited selves. The God who will not leave us orphaned keeps letting us know "what's next?" if we keep in touch. And it is this listening attitude which really leads to enjoying our home.

"Indeed, whoever labors to penetrate the secrets of reality with a humble and steady mind is, even unaware, being led by the hand of God."

from The Church in the Modern World,
document of the Second Vatican Council[5]

Sharing Our Home

Our whole book has focused on ourselves, and the inner life to be sought and found and enjoyed with the indwelling God. What of other people? Is not the kingdom to be created around us as well as within us? What of the neediest—those who have no homeland or no roof over their heads? What of those closer to us, who may be in need in any of dozens of ways (outer and inner)? Is this book one more product of the "New Narcissism," that trend of the late twentieth century that glorified self-help and I-centeredness?

An approach to spiritual growth that pulls one away from those in need and the needs of the earth is not about spiritual growth at all—at least not in the tradition of the western, monotheistic religions. It *is* narcissism, or just plain selfishness. One important point remains to be made so that the person who focuses on coming home has a complete picture, one with room for other people and their needs.

In both the Judaeo-Christian and eastern religious traditions, and according to Jung's thought as well, the person of most help to others is the person who has his or her own firm commitment to the spiritual life and its practices. The very best thing we can do for other people is to become the person *we* were born to become. If we care about collective change—social justice work or parish renewal or political campaigning or governmental reform—the approach described in these pages says: "there is no collective change without individual change."[6] Jung loved the Chinese story of the rainmaker, which is often quoted to illustrate this point.[7]

It's easy to see why this principle is so. As we develop, we care more and more deeply about others—not because we "should" or because we find our identity in serving. We care because, when our "I" is no longer the ruling force in our own lives and the Divine Power within is the director of our lives, we meet that same God in everyone else. With "Me" out of the way (not disposed of, just off to the side; remember the clear lens concept?), we realize that the

God whose dwelling place is at our own center dwells within our parents, our children, our co-workers, the stranger in the supermarket, the starving child in Africa and the refugee from the Far East or Central America. The boundary lines that separate the I-centered person from those in need dissolve. We become one with these other carriers of our God—and their need becomes our need. They are cut out of the same material as we are, impressed with the same mandalic pattern, reflections of ourselves.

In Chapter 3, we spoke of people being at differing places along the road to home. If we have discovered the wonderful inner world, we may long to share it with those we love—and yet, they may be in quite a different place than we are. Not all are supposed to embrace the inner journey—or, at least, not at the time we might like them to. This doesn't mean, of course, that we can't share what is so valuable to us—just that we must not try to forcefeed our own values (even the highest ones) onto others. Their conversion process is just that: *their* conversion process—not ours.

Persons often change when they meet someone who has gone one step further than they have. (Lawrence Kohlberg's work is indicative of this.) Marie-Louise von Franz writes of how the person who is devoted to individuation so often has a contagious effect on others:

> "It is as if a spark leaps from one to another. And this usually occurs when one has no intention of influencing others and often when one uses no words."[8]

There is a strong tradition among those who have embraced Jung's thought *against* anything resembling proselytizing; this is done both out of respect for the place in which others are—and, also, because the shiny person (or the person-becoming-shinier) does not *need* to proselytize. It is really an egocentric position to want to be The One With The Answers.

Those who are seeking first the kingdom of God become filled with the presence of God, and this just naturally overflows into personal witness and ministry of some form. We become more connected to others, and finer and finer instruments for whatever it is we do for others—listening, clothing and sheltering, praying for, teaching, loving. *What we do* is important; *who we are* is even more important.

Goodness must diffuse itself.

—*St. Thomas Aquinas*

"When I entered religious life fourteen years ago, we heard a lot in the novitiate about 'the heresy of good works.' That meant that someone could get so busy doing things that were good that she neglected her own spiritual life. I can still see our novice mistress, dear Sister Mary of the Cross, exhorting us to always put the Lord first and never allow ourselves to get away from the practices she taught us so well.

Well, that was then and now is now—and while I certainly agree with this teaching I received in formation, living it out has been something else. For instance, I work at the downtown office of our diocese in the religious education office. You don't really want to hear what my schedule was like last week—meetings six out of seven nights, traveling to give workshops to teachers three days (and, of course, the preparation for these sessions), planning the music for the annual diocesan convention, plus community meetings and our convent's participation in the block party where we live. . . that was just the beginning.

I'm exhausted. And my mind seems to be turning to seed, all in little bits and pieces. The good works abound and my inner life seems to be on hold, although I know God is with me. Sister Mary was right; this is heretical, and it's something I've explored with my spiritual director. Even though there may be no one else to do some of these things, I'm going to start saying 'no' (nicely) and get back to those one and a half hours I used to reserve each morning for prayer and Mass and dialogue with my dream figures and drawing. Then, I know I'll be ready to bring something to the people I meet the rest of the day.

Believe me, I've tried the merry-go-round, and it doesn't work! Here comes the new me—I'm never again going to feel guilty about taking time for my own needs. My new motto is: 'the quality of our outer life is only as good as the quality of our inner life'. What do you think of that?!''

Homes are most worth sharing when they're well cared for. Then, they are a blessing to other people.

Two Great Patterns

We come to the end of our book, but not the end of our journeys. As we have shared this time together, not one but two great archetypal patterns have emerged and continued to weave themselves throughout our pages.

The first is the pattern of our innermost home—the mandala. We have theologized it, found it in the pages of scripture, uncovered its still presence within—and without, drawn it, lived with it. The mandala is the most universal picture of the goal of spiritual growth, the answer to the questions "Where have I come from?" and "Where am I going?"

It is the basic pattern of
wholeness,
    totality,
        harmony,
            completeness.

It is the pattern imprinted on our soul that is striving for actualization, acting like a magnet to call us home.[9] It is God's perfection working in us; it is the great map of creation, a picture of the Kingdom.

And there is another pattern that has also threaded its way through this book, not as explicitly as our image of home but just as surely. It is the second great motif of our lives: the idea of the journey, of going somewhere, of pilgrimage, of the hero's quest. And it embodies the ideas of change and transformation, just as the mandala has the quality of permanence. This active, journeying pattern answers the question "What am I doing here?", and we experience it throughout our lives as

a normal way of living. . .
    that dies. . .
        and is reborn, changed, so that we are born again.

We know this pattern as the paschal mystery . . . and humans first learned about it from the world around them: the rising and "dying" of the sun each day, the birth and life and wintry death of

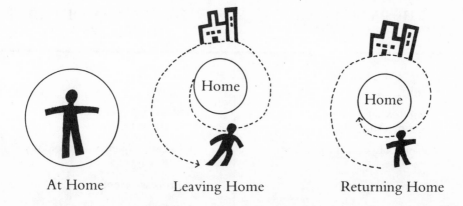

At Home   Leaving Home   Returning Home

the earth each year. Jesus lived it out, and used it in his parables: the grain of wheat, the Prodigal Son. The heroes of legends and the characters of fairy tales, those collective manifestations of a people, enact the same sequence. We learned to ritualize this pattern in liturgy and rites: in Baptism, and in the Eucharist, with its wheat and grape that have to die in order to be reborn.

Only after living the pattern on the outside, in these ways, did we also realize that it happens inwardly—just like the other megamotif, the mandala. The journeying pattern is about the birth of our consciousness or sense of self, the fruition of that, then the death of that ego-state as the center of our person, and the new life that we experience when reborn with God's life as our operating center. We also speak of it as metanoia, conversion.

So, here in our book we have encountered both patterns:

- the mandala, as HOME,

- the journey, as the COMING HOME. . .

and, how rich is our scriptural tradition in both these two great themes!

Sometimes we will feel one of them more operative in our lives, and at another time, the other will manifest itself more pointedly. We may see this as the balancing in us of the "feminine"—or waiting, expectant, embracing principle, and the "masculine"—or moving, doing, differentiating principle.[10]

251

THE PATTERN OF TOTALITY IS:	THE PATTERN OF THE JOURNEY IS:
• still	• active
• about what is already there— something old	• about what is yet to be— something new
• all-in-one, complete, static	• linear, sequential, unfolding, dynamic
• essence-oriented	• process-oriented
• acausal	• causal

We need to feel both operating within our lives.

We can look back to the map of spiritual growth we've been using and see both these motifs united. We are on the road, moving along—at the same time, that which is unchanging is at rest in the center, calling us to itself and becoming ever clearer as we draw near.

Both the mandala and the road or journey are part of our everyday lives; we meet them in symbols and in the events of our life all the time, and are drawn to them, because they are the primordial inner themes as well. And the inner "marriage" of the masculine and feminine energies results in balance and harmony in our souls.

So we leave you now with the wish that your inner home may, increasingly, be delighted in and enjoyed. It is the sanctuary of the living God, to whom we've so often prayed

". . . thy kingdom come . . . "

Asking for your prayers, we look forward to meeting all our known and unknown readers in the eternal home, after having sung *this* prayer here on earth.

"One thing I ask, this alone I seek:
To dwell in the house of the Lord all my days.
For one day within Your temple heals every day alone,
Oh Lord, bring me to Your dwelling."[11]

*Home is
where the heart is.*

Personal Journal Pages

I Will Walk in the Land of the Living

Throughout this book there has been an abundance of images—in word and picture—of the purpose of life here on earth. Taking time out and allowing it to come up from within me, can I write my own life story or parable? It may be about someone going home—or, it may take an entirely different form. (Fairy tales and stories from mythology and scriptural stories are good models for this sort of personal saga.) Perhaps the story will have three parts: a past, a present, and the future (my dreams and hopes).

"Once upon a time

"I would like to share with you the story of how I came to build my home. I have an acre of land in Mexico, not far from the southern border of the United States. This land came to me when I was almost fifty years old. I had never owned my own land before—it seems I had always cared for others' places. When I finally was able to have my own place, I knew I was there to stay.

At first I lived in a little shack with my animals. I planted a garden—all the things my father, who was a Spanish farmer, had taught me to grow—and I really was able to see the cycle of life. The food fed the animals, and they fertilized the land, which in turn produced more food. Soon all sorts of things were growing . . . I started with twelve amaryllis plants and now there are three hundred. It was fine for a while, but then—because my new life was coming in such abundance—I wanted to have a home that was worthy of it. The shack where I had been living didn't seem to be right for the garden that had blossomed and was just overflowing.

All the time I was thinking about how to live, I kept feeling that the house had already been built before—no, that's not it, it's more as if the blueprint of the house was already there inside of me, and I was just expressing in stone and wood and adobe what was already (invisibly) built. I never had a plan on paper—I didn't need one; the plan was already there.

Finally my home was built, and I now have a wife to share it with me. She is the final gift that was missing. We live by the sea, with the fruit trees and grapevines, and the goats and rabbits and dogs and doves. We are happy and at peace."

" . . . trailing clouds of glory do we come
    from God, who is our home . . .
Those shadowy recollections,
    . . . be they what they may,
Are yet the fountain light of all our day. . . ."

—*Ode on Intimations of Immortality*
from Recollections of Early Childhood,
William Wordsworth, 1807

In Summary

Coming Home has presented an approach to spiritual growth that is most easily pictured by the spiral "maps" of Chapter Four. In simplest form we could describe the process as

1. being at home, but not being aware of that
2. leaving home . . . then, turning around and
3. returning home, knowingly.

The developmental chart that follows shows the correspondence between the Christian language for this process and the Jungian language (using Dr. Jacobi's division of the individuation process, as referred to in note 8 of Chapter Four). It also gives us some of the scriptural images that tell about each stage of this growth process.

Although drawn in linear form, we should not imagine that everyone proceeds along a smooth growth path!—wouldn't that be nice! There are, so often, roadblocks and regressions all along the way. One may cease development at *any* point. Nothing about the soul can be described as neatly as a chart would have it . . . but it does give us an overview of the growth process.

It might be helpful to imagine the chart in the form of a tube, with the final right-hand column doubling back to the beginning; this developmental map—as the spiral pictures show us—isn't a one-way road or ladder, as it looks on paper, but a return to what has always been there, as the spiral map shows.

n.b. This chart is *not* age-specific; and one can stop at any point

The Life of the Soul	Beginnings ——→	Normal Life ——→
The Conversion Process: "I" and "Thou"	Little children are naturally in a state of union with God . . . although they may not know it. We celebrate this with **baptism.**	Mainstreamed into life of institution/group; celebrated in sacramental churches by **first penance and eucharist.** Part of church because of parents, then out of habit . . . or fear, or need for security. Unconscious identification with the collective group.
The Individuation Process: "I" and "Not-I" (or Self)	We are born with the "map" of totality already complete . . . in a pre-conscious unitive state. No sense of "I" or "me" (pre-ego). all is one ◯ (*participation mystique*) —no consciousness— Erich Neumann's UROBORIC STAGE,[1] after Uroborus, the ancient circular image of the serpent biting its own tail	*Individuation: Part 1* Sense of "I" (ego) begins to emerge from womb-like state, though still contained by it. (Neumann's MATRIARCHAL STAGE) 3 stages postulated by Kalff: • animal-vegetative (still very instinctual) • fighting to break out • adaptation to the collective (Neumann's PATRIARCHAL STAGE) *May* make it = healthy ego ("the hero") OR *May not* make it = ego remains weak, and compensates by defenses (Kunkel)[2] and/or seeking new substitute "womb"
The Story of Salvation (Salvation History)	Creation of the World	
	Paradise Prodigal son at home	Kingdom of Israel —— Promised Land —— Jerusalem, the holy city —— Goes away Grain of wheat —— "I live . . ." "The people who

1. See Erich Neumann's *The Child* (New York: G.P. Putnam's Sons, 1973). Neumann has written at length on the way in which this stage theory differs in the lives of men and of women (in German; translated into English by Rebecca Jacobson in *Spring 1959*, New York: The Analytical Psychology Club of New York, Inc.). Were our simple chart to be amplified, it would include such distinctions; as it is, this chart is the basic "map" for people of either gender. There are, also, Buddhist systems which parallel this spiral map. See, for example, Lama Govinda's lectures on Pali Buddhism (early Indian) in *The Psychological Attitude of Early Buddhist Philosophy* (New York: Samuel Weiser, 1974). The Mahayana Buddhists use three descriptive terms

Death to that Life ——→	New Life (Completed in Eternity) ⚹☉
Separation from Faith of Child: 1. leave . . . "that's not for me" and/or 2. "there's got to be more . . . " A turning around (PURGATIVE STAGE of old texts) (Wm. James & Kelsey suggest that we may skip this phase: the "once-born" or O'Collins' "smooth evolvers"; most, however, are "twice-born.")	**Adult Conversion/2nd Journey:** (ILLUMINATIVE & UNITIVE stages) *Personal* relationship with God sought, leading to intimate union of love. Church ambiguous about how to celebrate this! In *some* views, **confirmation** (as a recommitment to one's baptismal vows) could celebrate adult conversion.

Individuation: Part 2

The Old Way No Longer Works:
 1. Crisis leads to "I need help/change" (i.e., ego not strong enough to meet the crisis, can no longer control)
 (One feels like one is being "cooked" or in a furnace . . . which can burn one to a bitter crisp, *or* refine one to gold. In one case, give up and regress—in the other, go through the crisis, find higher power within)
          and/or
 2. Respond to inner call to self- (ego-) transcendence, as (capital S) Self/image of God makes its presence felt (Jung's "religious instinct" is Self longing for *re*union).
	Rearrangement of the Personality:
	 Center shifts from ego to Self.
	 (Edinger's INTEGRATIVE STAGE)[3]
	 Ego no longer in charge, but remains strong—is servant/channel/mirror of true Center (which has always been there).
	 Ego-Self axis established.
	
	 A return to the unitive consciousness of childhood . . . but this time, aware of it (conscious, intentional).
	      All is one . . . again.
	 (Neumann's GREAT INDIVIDUAL)

Collapse of the Kingdom(s) ————	The Kingdom is Within
Paradise lost ————————	Paradise regained
In Exile ("Captive Israel")————	Return to Promised Land
(earlier: the desert) ————	("Ransomed Israel")
Jerusalem destroyed ————	The new Jerusalem, Heaven
from home (pigs!) ————	Returns home
buried in ground ————	sprouts and grows ("new creation," "born again")
"now, not I . . . " ————	"but Christ lives in me"
"I must decrease . . . " ————	"that He may increase"
walk in darkness . . . " ————	"have seen a great light"
"Heart of stone," "hardness of ♥" ———	"become as little children"

ONE CAN MOVE ALONG: *a. With the group or collective*   *b. On the solo path*   *c. Both (b. has priority)*

Note that throughout this book and the chart there are two circular diagrams, not to be confused:
• the spiral pictures, which are the map of the growth process itself;
• the mandalic pictures, which show the soul as it *goes through* the growth process and in their simplest form show the beginning and end of the growth process.

From: *Coming Home: A Handbook for Exploring the Sanctuary Within.* Copyright © 1986 by Betsy Caprio and Thomas M. Hedberg, S.D.B. Used by permission.

that parallel Neumann's: "the person of little understanding," "the person of normal understanding," and "the person of superior understanding."

2. See Dora Kalff reference, notes for Chapter Seven, and Kunkel reference, notes for Chapter Four.

3. See Dr. Edinger's outline in issue No. 1 of *Quadrant* (N.Y.: C.G. Jung Foundation for Analytical Psychology, 1968).

NOTES

INTRODUCTION:
1. Antoine de Saint-Exupéry, *Wind, Sand and Stars* (New York: Harcourt, Brace and World, Inc. 1967), p. 13-14.

CHAPTER TWO:
1. Genesis 2:8-19.
2. Genesis 13:14.
3. In his *Dictionary of the Bible* (Milwaukee: Bruce Publishing Co., 1965), John McKenzie, S. J. gives this as a possible modern interpretation of the word "Israel," while noting that its usual etymological translation suggests "one who wrestles with God" or "one who contends against God."
4. I Chronicles 22:6.
5. Isaiah 49:15-16.
6. Revelation 21:10-27.
7. There are many representations of the holy city in art and music, one of the most powerful being Alan Hovhaness' *The Holy City*, a short piece for orchestra based on liturgical themes from the Armenian church. It could be a powerful adjunct to the imagery of this chapter.
8. A modern dreamer shares her version of the holy city in *Dreams of a Woman*, Sheila Moon's autobiography (Boston: Sigo Press, 1983), p. 105. Also helpful in stirring our imagination is Raymond Moody's gathering of reports of the afterlife experience; the three qualities most often cited by those who have "been there" are 1) seeing light and vivid colors, 2) a sense of peace, and 3) reassurance that death was not fearful but liberating. See *Life After Life* (Mockingbird Books, 1975).

CHAPTER THREE:
1. Morton Kelsey is one who uses "soul" and "psyche" interchangeably. See *Psychological Types*, C. G. Jung, Volume 6 of the Collected Works (Princeton: Princeton University Press, 1971; originally published 1921), paragraph 797 ff. for Jung's conceptual difference between the two.
2. William James is a basic source on religious experience; see, particularly, the references to his views in *Companions on the Inner Way* by Morton Kelsey (New York: Crossroad Publishing Co., 1983) under Kelsey's comments on conversion, p. 192 ff. Gerald O'Collins' approach to conversion is titled *The Second Journey: Spiritual Awareness and the Mid-Life Crisis* (New York: Paulist Press, 1978).
3. In *Psychology and Alchemy*, Volume 12 of the Collected Works (Princeton: Princeton University Press, 1953; originally published 1944), C. G. Jung gives a dream example of such an inner garden or mini-Eden. See paragraph 154.

4. Isaiah 35:8:10.

5. Isaiah 35:1-2, 55:12, 65:25.

6. The quotation is from 14th century English mystic Richard Rolle, a hermit from Yorkshire, who wrote *The Fire of Love.* Quoted in *The Fire and the Cloud*, David A. Fleming, S.M. (New York: Paulist Press, 1978), p. 188.

7. Cf. the story of the Samaritan woman at the well, John 4:5-42.

8. Isaiah 55:1.

9. C. G. Jung explored the symbolism of the fish as an image of that which lives in the unconscious in great depth. See *Aion*, Volume 9ii of his Collected Works (Princeton: Princeton University Press, 1959; originally published in 1951).

10. In *Christo-Psychology* (New York: Crossroad Publishing Co., 1982), Morton Kelsey reaffirms the value of the collective path (see page 65), reminding us that not everyone is called to explore the way to the kingdom in an individual way.

11. Thomas Howard's book *Hallowed Be This House* (Wheaton, IL: Harold Shaw Publishers, 1979; originally published as *Splendor in the Ordinary*) is filled with simple reflections on the sacramental aspects of each room of the house.

12. From *The Mathnawi*, a thirteenth century poem by Maulana Jalalu'ddin Rumi, Reynold A. Nicholson, translator (London, 1934).

CHAPTER FOUR:

1. Jean-Marie Déchanet, O.S.B., *Christian Yoga* (New York: Harper and Row, 1960). This book has become a classic in the movement to rejoin the too-long-separated soul and body.

2. See how the Declaration on Religious Freedom in *The Documents of Vatican II*, Walter M. Abbott, S.J., general editor (New York: The America Press, 1966) restates for the Roman Catholic Church its tradition of belief in the primacy of conscience.

3. The basic Jungian reference on development of the ego is the work of Jung's disciple Erich Neumann, *The Origins and History of Consciousness* (Princeton: Princeton University Press, 1954). Neumann refers to the "paradise state" as the uroboric state, named for the tail-biting serpent, Uroboros—the perfect self-contained circle. See the chart at the end of the book for further amplification of the development of the ego, and Neumann's stage theory.

4. This is one of the most encouraging thoughts imaginable! In *The Way of Individuation* (New York: Harcourt Brace and World, Inc., 1967), Jolande Jacobi (who left her native Hungary and studied with Jung during the second World War) has a skillfully-etched chapter on this religious function of the psyche. She quotes another author's phrase, "God does not leave (people) in peace," but—we would say— continues to call them.

Jung speaks of the goal-directed nature of the psyche in many places. See, for example, paragraph 328 of *Psychology and Alchemy*, where Jung discusses, "images of the goal . . . which the psychic process, being 'purposive,' apparently sets up of its own accord . . . "

5. The four egocentric adaptations mentioned by the story-teller come from the work of Fritz Kunkel, *How Character Develops*, authored in 1940 with Roy Dickerson. They have been more recently popularized by his pupil John A. Sanford, who excerpts Kunkel's major thought in *Fritz Kunkel: Selected Writings* (New York: Paulist Press, 1984), and in Sanford's excellent tape series *The Path to Wholeness* (Kansas City, MO: NCR Credence Cassettes). In these recorded talks, Sanford focuses on a gap in Jung's thought—the egocentricity of the ego.

6. Morton Kelsey stresses this impersonal nature of the Self in several of his works, comparing it to the impersonality of "I Am Who Am."

7. The useful concept of the "ego-Self axis" comes from Erich Neumann, and has been made better known through the work of Edward Edinger. See his *Ego and Archetype* (New York: G. P. Putnam's Sons, 1972), Chapter 2.

This book also has a valuable section on the role of the collective (the "group journey") in Chapter 3, and in a more recent book, *The Creation of Consciousness* (Toronto: Inner City Books, 1984), Dr. Edinger makes a valuable distinction between being *related to* a religion—or any collective—and being *contained in* it. Containment is unconscious; we allow the religion to carry our connection to the archetypal realm for us; relatedness, on the other hand, is a conscious appreciation of a faith because we ourselves have encountered the numinous, and now find that connection underlined for us by the liturgy and stories of the religion. Containment in a collective and relatedness to it are two very different things.

8. See, for example, *The Way of Individuation*, Chapter 4.

9. This well-known Eliot quotation is from his *Four Quartets* (1943).

10. See *Memories, Dreams, Reflections* (New York: Random House, Inc., 1973), page 196 ff. In this, his autobiography, Jung talks about how the insight that everything points toward the center gave him stability and inner peace.

11. In one of his most evocative analogies, Jung speaks of this "shy animal" quality of the ego on its way home, being pulled by that central force; *Psychology and Alchemy*, paragraph 326. Neumann's name for that tendency is centroversion.

12. Other basics to add to this might include the rest of the Sanford and Kelsey writings, *Spiritual Pilgrims* by John Welch and *The Woman Sealed in the Tower* by Betsy Caprio (both, Paulist Press), Wallace Clift's *Jung and Christianity* (Crossroad), the excellent March/April 1984 issue of *New Catholic World* on "Jung and Religion," and the materials for four years of small group study from Centerpoint.

CHAPTER FIVE:

1. "In the darkness of the unconscious a treasure lies hidden . . . " says Jung in *Symbols of Transformation*, Volume 5 of the Collected Works (Princeton: Princeton University Press, 1956; originally published, 1912), paragraph 510.

2. *The Twelve Dancing Princesses*, Grimm fairy tale number 133, also is known as *The Dancing Shoes*. A most interesting study of it appears in a *Quadrant* article by Ann and Barry Ulanov (Vol. 11, No. 2, Winter 1978).

3. See J. E. Cirlot's *A Dictionary of Symbols* (New York: Philosophical Library, 1962), page 334, for amplification on twelve-ness.

4. Jung cautions against "believing that the unconscious always knows best" in "On the Nature of Dreams" in Volume 8 of the Collected Works, *The Structure and Dynamics of the Psyche* (Princeton: Princeton University Press, 1960; originally published, 1945), paragraph 568.

5. For more information on synchronicity, Jean Shinoda Bolen's book, *The Tao of Psychology* (New York: Harper and Row, 1979) is an excellent place to begin. The basic reference is Jung's essay, *Synchronicity: An Acausal Connecting Principle* found in Volume 8 of the Collected Works.

6. C. G. Jung, *Psychology and Alchemy*, paragraph 442.

7. The figure of the psychopomp roams all through Jung's commentaries on the old alchemical texts. See the several references in *Psychology and Alchemy* and the frequent ap-

pearances of Mercurius in *The Psychology of the Transference* in Volume 16 of his Collected Works, *The Practice of Psychotherapy* (Princeton: Princeton University Press, 1946) and all through *Alchemical Studies*, Volume 13 of the Collected Works (Princeton: Princeton University Press, 1967; articles in this volume originally published between 1929 and 1954) and *Mysterium Coniunctionis*, Volume 14 of the Collected Works (Princeton: Princeton University Press, 1963).

8. The basics are Morton Kelsey's two dreaming books: *Dreams: A Way To Listen to God* (Paulist Press, 1978) and *God, Dreams and Revelation* (Augsburg Publishing, 1968) and John Sanford's pair: *Dreams and Healing* (Paulist, 1978) and *Dreams: God's Forgotten Language* (Lippincott, 1968). There are several fine books published since these four laid the groundwork, most notably *Dreams and Spiritual Growth* by Louis M. Savary, Patricia H. Berne and Strephon K. Williams (Paulist, 1984).

9. One of the best descriptions of active imagination techniques is in June Singer's book *Boundaries of the Soul* (Garden City: Doubleday, 1972), Chapter 12. See also Sanford's *Healing and Wholeness* (New York: Paulist Press, 1977), pp. 140 ff, and Barbara Hannah's work on the same subject, *Encounters with the Soul: Active Imagination as Developed by C. G. Jung* (Boston: Sigo Press, 1981).

10. In *King Saul, the Tragic Hero* (Mahwah, NJ: Paulist Press, 1985), John Sanford compares analytical psychology and archetypal psychology in terms of the former's focus on the unity of the psyche in the Self, and the latter's emphasis on the multiplicity of images in the psyche (see page 57). Hillman's focus on the images within leads him to language like " . . . the feeling of being loved by the images . . . imaginal love" (from *Archetypal Psychology*. Dallas: Spring Publications, Inc., 1983, p. 14).

11. Two very complete books on journal keeping are Morton Kelsey's *Adventure Inward* (Minneapolis: Augsburg Publishing Co., 1980) and *Keeping Your Personal Journal* by George Simons (New York: Paulist Press, 1978).

12. On the spiritual companion, see Morton Kelsey's *Companions on the Inner Way* (New York: Crossroad, 1983), *Spiritual Friend* by Tilden Edwards (New York: Paulist, 1980) and *Soul Friend* by Kenneth Leech (New York: Harper and Row, 1977).

13. As much as Jung's thought on individuation has to teach us about spiritual growth, for the believer it is not a complete approach. See the companion book to *Coming Home, Coming Home: A Manual for Spiritual Direction* for omissions in the psychological stance, which of necessity must treat what can be measured rather than matters of faith—the province of religion. See also the excellent article in the March/April 1984 issue of *New Catholic World* by Robert T. Sears, titled "Individuation and Spiritual Growth."

14. On space apart, Sören Kierkegaard is often quoted on the bad press solitude has been given, because of its primary use as a punishment for criminals. See p. 198 of *Fear and Trembling and the Sickness Unto Death* (New York: Doubleday and Co., 1954). We might add to criminals " . . . and for children."

CHAPTER SIX:

1. More often phrased as "anything rejected from the psyche becomes hostile."

2. For more information on the shadow see *Man and His Symbols* by Jung and his colleagues (London: Aldus Books, 1964), page 166; *Shadow and Evil in Fairy Tales* by Marie-Louise von Franz (Dallas: Spring Publications, 1974) and *Make Friends with Your Shadow* by William A. Miller (Minneapolis: Augsburg Publishing House, 1981).

3. Jung and his followers speak of "mana-personalities," those figures with that nu-

minosity that makes them larger than life. The dream figure is of this sort. A Polynesian concept of spiritual power, mana is invisible but very powerful. See *Two Essays on Analytical Psychology* by C. G. Jung, Volume 7 of the Collected Works (Princeton: Princeton University Press, 1953; originally published 1917 and 1928) paragraph 388 ff.

4. From "Concerning Mandala Symbolism" in *The Archetypes and the Collective Unconscious,* Volume 9i of C. G. Jung's Collected Works (Princeton: Princeton University Press, 1959), paragraph 712.

5. This episode has been shown to patients in mental institutions since its first showing in 1966, to make the point that shadow sides of our nature are essential to our totality. See also *Star Trek: Good News in Modern Images* by Betsy Caprio (Mission, KS: Andrews and McMeel, 1978), page 60.

6. In *The Kingdom Within*, John Sanford helps us understand the inner meaning of the famous "when I was hungry . . . " verses from Matthew 25 (Philadelphia: Lippincott Co., 1970). See, especially, p. 183, and all of Chapter 6, "The Inner Adversary."

7. From "Concerning Mandala Symbolism". *op. cit.*, paragraphs 660 and 620.

8. From a recollection of Barbara Hannah of a conversation between herself and Jung.

9. In *Jungian Theory and Therapy*, Tom Laughlin makes a strong case for not losing Jung's focus on the instinctual nature of the psyche, especially in the creation of the archetypes and the images of them (Los Angeles: Panarion Press, 1982).

10. Origen's quote is from *In Leviticum Homiliae*, V, 2.

11. Fortunately, we seem to be nearing the end of our denial-of-the-body-in-the-name-of-God (who became human). One of the promising signs is the publication of books like Joan Ohanneson's *And They Felt No Shame: Christians Reclaim Their Sexuality* (Minneapolis: Winston Press, 1983).

12. *Compassion* by Matthew Fox (Minneapolis: Winston Press, 1979), page 165. Irish and Welsh (Celtic) hagiography offers an especially rich lore on saints and animals, a carryover from the old nature religion of the Celtic peoples. For example, there was the stag which allowed St. Cainnech to use its antlers as a bookrest. Throughout the illuminated manuscripts of the Celtic church, animals leap, fly and crawl with abandon, as if to say, "We're part of the Good News too!" See, too, James Hillman on "animal faith" (e.g. *Inter Views*. New York: Harper & Row, 1983, p. 90).

13. Centerpoint, 33 Main St., #302, Nashua, NH 03060.

14. See note 10, Chapter Four.

15. "Homeward Bound," words and music by Paul Simon (on Columbia Record CS9363, titled *Parsley, Sage, Rosemary and Thyme*).

CHAPTER SEVEN:

1. "Land of Rest" is what is known as a "white spiritual," a folk hymn from yesteryear often set to a secular tune (usually modal). The roots of the melody for this hymn are folk air strains of Scotland and Northern England, and it is similar to one of the collected melodies for "Lord Thomas and Fair Ellinor" (Child Ballad #73) and "Little Musgrave and Lady Barnard" (Child #81), in their American versions as collected by Cecil Sharp. "Land of Rest" is Ionian in mode and hexatonic in scale. The black spiritual, "Swing Low, Sweet Chariot" is related to this folk-hymn, as a comparison of their melodies will show. Early collector Annabel Morris Buchanan of Virginia learned this from her grandmother. A second set of lyrics set to the same tune dates from the 16th century and is making a reap-

pearance in today's hymnals and missalettes; it is titled *Jerusalem, My Happy Home* and echoes the same sentiment: the longing for home.

2. Thomas Merton, *Contemplation in a World of Action*, (New York: Doubleday and Co., Inc., 1971), page 216.

3. "Our House" by Graham Nash (on Atlantic Records' title *Déjà Vu*).

4. See *Memories, Dreams, Reflections*, page 195 ff. and "Concerning Mandala Symbolism," paragraph 634.

5. *Memories, Dreams, Reflections*, page 196.

6. See John Sanford's *The Invisible Partners* (New York: Paulist Press, 1980) for the best treatment of the feminine and masculine in a personality. Also, B. Caprio, *op. cit.*

7. Two valuable works on mandalas in general are *Mandala* by José and Miriam Argüelles (Berkeley: Shambala Publications, Inc., 1972) and *Pathway to Ecstasy: The Way of the Dream Mandala* by Patricia Garfield (New York: Holt, Rinehart and Winston, 1979).

8. *Ibid.*, p. 195.

9. Jung wrote in *Psychology and Religion: West and East*, Volume 11 of the Collected Works, (Princeton: Princeton University Press, 1958) that "since olden times, the circle with a center has been a symbol for the Deity, illustrating the wholeness of God . . . " (paragraph 418). The squaring of the circle is described in *Man and His Symbols* by Aniela Jaffé, who notes that in our day—as reflected in the art of our time—the two forms of circle and square are usually *not* connected, illustrating the separation of persons from God (see page 249; also Dr. von Franz' comments on page 215). The squared circle may also be seen as the original (circular) garden of Paradise combined with the more conscious (squared) heavenly city of *Revelation*.

10. See Chapter Four, "The Universal Language of the House" in Marc Olivier's wonderful book *The Psychology of the House* (London: Thames and Hudson, Ltd., 1972); also Patricia Garfield, *op. cit.*

11. From "Flying Saucers: A Modern Myth" in *Civilization in Transition*, Volume 10 of the Collected Works of C. G. Jung (Princeton: Princeton University Press, 1964), paragraph 803.

12. From Jung's Introduction to the Chinese *Book of Consciousness and Life*, found in "Commentary on *The Secret of the Golden Flower*" in *Alchemical Studies*, paragraphs 18-20.

13. *Sandplay: Mirror of a Child's Psyche*, Dora Kalff (San Francisco: The Browser Press, 1971).

14. An excellent aid to constructing one's own mandala are the tapes on "Integration and the Shadow" by Robert Johnson (Pecos, NM: Dove Publications).

15. See "A Study in the Process of Individuation" with a series of mandalas drawn by a woman patient of C. G. Jung. They show clearly the healing power of the mandala; it grows more complete as its creator grows more complete. In *The Archetypes and the Collective Unconscious*, figures 2-24.

16. "Rebuild My Temple" by John Michael Talbot, in the album *Troubadour of the Great King* (Sparrow Records, Inc., Canoga Park, CA, 1981).

17. Robert Johnson provides us with the quintessential treatment of romantic and other kinds of love in *We* (New York: Harper and Row, 1983).

CHAPTER EIGHT:

1. Daniel 12:2.

2. *The Creation of Consciousness* is a thought-provoking work, the mature fruit of one

271

of Jung's most creative and brilliant interpreters. Like Teilhard de Chardin, Dr. Edinger's work takes us to a reconciliation of science and religion. The book also contains a reflection on Jung's controversial essay *Answer to Job*, which tends to view evil in a way incongruent with Christian tradition. See also *Sparks of Light* by Zalman M. Schachter and Edward Hoffman, which tells us about counseling in the Hasidic tradition (Boulder, CO: Shambhala Publications, Inc., 1983).

3. Two good sources of angelology are *A Dictionary of Angels* by Gustav Davison (New York: The Free Press, 1967) and *Angels* by Peter Lamborn Wilson (London: Thames and Hudson, Ltd., 1980). For more information on the intriguing Islamic idea of the angels as the archetypes of human beings—or our "doubles"—see *Creative Imagination in the Sufism of Ibn 'Arabi* by Henry Corbin (Princeton: Princeton University Press, 1969) esp. p. 222.

4. Throughout his life's work of researching "self-actualizing" and "self-transcending" persons, Abraham Maslow noted more than once their transcendence of various dichotomies. See, for example, page 304 of *The Farther Reaches of Human Nature* (New York: The Viking Press, 1971), where he talks about the work-play dichotomy . . . and how both can be seen as two parts of a whole. The theme is typically Jungian; the balance of opposites is a key concept in C. G. Jung's psychology.

5. *The Gospel According to Thomas*, Logion 22.

6. "A Study in the Process of Individuation," note 141.

7. Letter of C. G. Jung, April 23, 1949, in *C. G. Jung: Letters, Vol. I*, Gerhard Adler, ed., with Aniela Jaffé (Princeton: Princeton University Press, 1953).

8. This is a somewhat different view from Jung's, a summary of which can be found in *C. G. Jung, Emma Jung and Toni Wolff: A Collection of Remembrances*, Ferne Jensen, ed. (San Francisco, 1982). Ours is closer to that of C. S. Lewis, who says we are "between the angels who are our eldest brothers and the beasts who are our jesters, servants and playfellows" (*That Hideous Strength*, p. 378). In *We* Robert Johnson writes about the Cathari ("the pure"); see page 69 ff.

9. Isaiah 40:31.

10. Psalm 55:6.

11. "Commentary on *The Secret of the Golden Flower*," paragraph 17.

12. See also Matthew 22:30: "The elect will be like the angels in heaven."

CHAPTER NINE:

1. Matthew 7:24.

2. Psalm 137:5-6.

3. A good introduction to Jung's typology is in *Man and His Symbols*, p. 58 ff. See also *From Image to Likeness: A Jungian Path in the Gospel Journey* by W. Harold Grant, Magdala Thompson and Thomas E. Clarke (New York: Paulist Press, 1983), which has valuable suggestions on developing each of the four functions (although it is a little too locked into age-specificity to reflect Jung's thought perfectly). Also, Chapter 7 of *Christo-Psychology*, titled "Psychological Types and the Religious Way" and written by Barbara Kelsey gives a clear presentation of this often confusing subject.

4. Revelation 3:15-16.

5. *Gaudium et Spes*, found in *The Documents of Vatican II*.

6. See one of many mentions of this point in C. G. Jung's work in "A Study in the Process of Individuation," paragraph 618.

7. An elaboration on the story is to be found in Chapter Nine of *Knowing Woman* by Irene de Castillejo (New York: G. P. Putnam's Sons, 1973).

8. In *Man and His Symbols*, page 224.

9. See *Psychology and Alchemy*, paragraph 325.

10. See the Appendix of *The Woman Sealed in the Tower*. Also, page 114 ff. of *The Psychology of the House*, which speaks of masculine and feminine styles of house construction. The former are the pyramidal, steepled buildings that reach up to heaven; the latter, flat, open-roofed houses, often with a central courtyard containing a pool or fountain in which the sky is reflected. "The Muslim soul," writes the author on page 56, "sought union with heaven by opening itself to it, rather than by trying to reach up to it."

11. Psalms 27:4 and 84:10, set to music by the St. Louis Jesuits.

My Favorite Pictures and Quotes about HOME

My Favorite Pictures and Quotes about HOME

My Favorite Pictures and Quotes about HOME

My Favorite Pictures and Quotes about HOME

About the Authors

Betsy Caprio is director of the Center for Sacred Psychology in Culver City, California. She holds an M.A. in Transpersonal Education from Beacon College, Washington, D.C., and is a member of the Association for Transpersonal Psychology. Among her published books are *Experiments in Prayer*, *Experiments in Growth*, and *The Woman Sealed in the Tower*.

Thomas M. Hedberg, S.D.B. is a spiritual director, a therapist and founder of Youth Encounter Spirit, an international retreat movement. He holds an M.A. in psychology from Loyola University of Los Angeles and, like Ms. Caprio, he has attended the C.G. Jung Institute in Zurich, Switzerland.

A companion volume for parents, prayer partners,
retreat directors, formation directors, pastoral counselors,
psychologists, therapists, religious educators:

COMING HOME
A Manual for Spiritual Direction
By Betsy Caprio and Thomas M. Hedberg

Available from your bookstore or from
Paulist Press
997 Macarthur Boulevard
Mahwah, N.J. 07430